Early Money:

A Brief Introduction to the World of High Finance and the Opportunities to Transition from College Student to Investment Banker

ISBN-13:
978-1983706868

ISBN-10:
1983706868

Acknowledgements

Authors RJ Ammons and Morgan Eldon would like to thank the many mentors, friends, and family who have guided them along their respective career paths.

RJ would like to specifically thank his parents, Rob and Chris Ammons, for always loving him.

Morgan would like to thank his parents for reading the entirety of this work, and his girlfriend for watching over the final hours of its completion.

Both RJ and Morgan would like to thank Billy, Tom, Johnny, Konrad[*], and Sam, for serving as both friends and mentors.

---

[*] Even though he has no holiday cheer and failed to invite Morgan to his recent Christmas party.

Table of Contents

Preface

RJ Ammons and Morgan Eldon, the authors of this book, first met at Harvard College when they were 18 and 19 years old, respectively. While Morgan Eldon started college with plans to become a fiction writer, RJ Ammons started college with plans to become a lawyer. Throughout their years at Harvard, they both learned about and became interested in various careers in the financial services industry, a field that they had known little about before attending Harvard.

The purpose of this book is simple: we aim to inform college students of entry-level positions in the financial services industry. Specifically, we aim to shed light on entry-level roles at investment banks. We have chosen to focus on banking because it is the most popular path for freshly minted college graduates, and entry-level positions in banking do not require specific educational requirements beyond those satisfied by a bachelor's degree.

Additionally, we have included an introduction to venture capital and private equity. Although there are relatively few entry-level positions available for college graduates, our experience has shown that positions can be successfully secured for those who have prior experience in finance via internships. These industries are much more private and typically do not openly recruit college graduates.

RJ's Note

When I arrived at Harvard College, I had the slightest idea about the opportunities available in the financial services industry. I had come to college with the plan of going to law school, not out of any particular desire to practice law[1], but because it sounded like a more palatable path than those to careers in medicine and engineering. Being unaware of other options, I had settled on law school, until I was informed of the opportunities available in the financial services industry, specifically, jobs in the **investment banking divisions**[2] of **bulge bracket banks**[3].

Through many long hours of mentorship, online research, numerous internships / jobs, participation in finance clubs while at Harvard, and helping many students secure employment in the financial services industry, I believe I have reached a point in my life in which I have a thorough understanding of the opportunities available to freshly minted college graduates from top-tier American universities. To help future generations of students interested in finance, Morgan and I have put together this short book that explains a few of the different entry-level positions in the financial services industry.

Of course, the world of finance is complex, so not every generalization we have laid out is applicable to all banks / firms. These generalizations are simply

---

[1] Over the last year, I have developed a strong desire to become a lawyer. Although I have worked in the financial services industry for the last few years, I believe that law school is indeed the next step in my individual journey.

[2] The investment banking division of an investment bank is distinct from its markets division (sometimes called "sales and trading") and internal functions divisions. Bankers in the investment banking division work on deals that include material nonpublic information (MNPI).

[3] "Bulge bracket" is a term referring to the group of investment banks with the largest balance sheets. In investment banking deals, the final print notice lists the name of the bank with the responsibility of securities distribution in bulging letters. This gave rise to the term "bulge bracket."

attempts to shine light on some of the bigger picture concepts Morgan and I have developed over time. If you are reading this book, you are most likely considering a career in finance. If that is the case, I wish you luck on all future endeavors, regardless of your career decision.

Sincerely,

RJ Ammons

Morgan's Note

After my first year at Harvard college, I had succeeded in tearing my hip labrum, fracturing three of the bones in my right foot, and getting my first B-. For a high school valedictorian and track star with near perfect SAT scores (lost 10 points on the writing section), these were not the achievements I had expected to attain after my first two semesters at the world's leading institution of higher education. In the summer between my freshman and sophomore years, I worked four part-time jobs to afford my shared apartment in Cambridge while training (on hobbled legs) for cross country and writing my first (still and hopefully forever unpublished) novel.

That summer, my prior aspirations to become a fiction writer were both satisfied and disappointed. I learned that although I could complete a novel I was proud of within a 3-month period, I had not added anything that new to the world. Yes, I had generated a piece of literature perhaps more interesting than what a million monkeys with a million typewriters could have produced over, say, 100 years, but I had not done more than put the thoughts of a cocky 19-year-old with no real wisdom to paper. I did not have any real-life experience, did not have any real marketable skills, and did not have any real money in my bank account.

This fiction stuff was fugazi. I found that I wanted to do something that 1) had a meaningful impact on the world around me 2) taught me transferable skills 3) interested me and challenged me on an intellectual level and 4) paid me enough to support a comfortable lifestyle. Then, as now, I saw certain paths within the financial field as affording me an opportunity to satisfy these four objectives. After chairing Harvard College's oldest investment club, acting as PM in the world's most elite undergraduate hedge fund, and working on a trading floor for almost a year, I can say for sure that the financial industry does offer meaningful work for self-motivated and tenacious individuals. This is not to say that every role within the field offers the same benefits and verticals—in fact, I found my first job to be a very poor fit for me, and I spent an amount of time reevaluating my career path before deciding to reenter finance in a research role.

As someone who has changed education and career paths more than once in his 23 years, I can honestly say that this field is not for everyone. If you love organic chemistry, working in lab, and interned for a cancer research institute, you should probably go into medicine or advanced biological/chemical study. You will be compensated financially and spiritually much more than you will be if you force yourself into a field which often requires staring at excel spreadsheets and pitch books for double-digit-hour shifts. If you're a tech whiz who programmed his or her first iOS app at age 12 and you get your highs off drinking Red Bull and coding until 4:30AM, you should probably go work for Google. If you're like a good friend of mine and read books on option pricing and were an HFT-trading firm's best intern at age 20, finance is probably for you. Whoever you are and whatever path you choose, I urge you to read this book in its entirety—if what we explain sounds enticing, go for it. If what you read makes you want to reconsider the industry, that's great too. You won't have wasted precious time applying to jobs you never really wanted. Either way, I wish you good luck, and hope you will find this book to be a first guide on the path to your future.

Best of luck,
Morgan Eldon

Structure of the Book

Part One: Defining the Financial Services Industry and Knowing Your Role in Context

Although the financial services industry can be defined to include a broad scope of work, we will be using the following definition for the purposes of this book: *the financial services industry aims to assist individuals, corporations, and governments with decisions relating to the allocation of capital and risk.*

We believe that it is of the utmost importance that a high-level understanding of the financial services industry be achieved before discussing entry-level positions. This comes from a broader belief that we hold: to properly understand any system, first either a top-down and bottom-up approach must be taken, and our experience has shown that it is much easier to start with the top-down approach for explaining broadly the world of finance. In Part One, we focus exclusively on this definition, and show how investment banks primarily assist in the process of allocating capital between parties.

Part Two: Divisions of a Bulge Bracket Investment Bank

In Part Two, we explain the functions of an investment bank. We break apart a hypothetical, bulge-bracket bank and explain the various roles within the firm. Each chapter explains a particular division of an investment bank, and we conclude each chapter with popular exit strategies following a one- or two-year analyst program at a bulge bracket bank.

Part Three: An Introduction to Venture Capital and Private Equity

Part Three introduces and focuses on opportunities in venture capital & private equity. There are typically fewer entry-level positions available in these areas, but some do exist.

Part Four: The Path

Part Four is a summary of what we have talked about and our explanation of the financial career path for those graduating from elite colleges and universities.

Part Five: Job Information

Part Five is an overview of the recruiting process, strategies we recommend to those considering a career in The Financial Services Industry, and a template of the resume format we personally use.

Part One: Defining the Financial Services Industry and Knowing your Role in Context

Google   why silos

why silos **are bad**

Part One: Defining the Financial Services Industry and Knowing Your Role in Context

In a capitalist society, all commercial firms attempt to achieve an accounting profit in the course of ordinary business dealings[4]. Some firms specialize in helping commercial firms achieve this profit: usually by providing **investment capital**[5] or advising firms on **strategic and operational decisions**[6] that can either lead to additional profit or a return to profitability. The collection of firms that specialize in helping other firms achieve additional profit are firms in the financial services industry. *The financial services industry aims to assist individuals, corporations, and governments with decisions relating to the allocation of capital and risk.* We believe that helping corporations, governments, and individuals in the process of capital allocation is the role of sell-side and buy-side financiers (Chapter 1).

---

[4] We will be focusing on for-profit firms.

[5] Investment capital is money to be used for the purpose of making more money.

[6] Strategic decisions relate to broad concepts, such as Apple's decision to release the iPod. Operational decisions relate to day-to-day activities and logistics of the firm, such as a decision to change the form of primary communication from *verbal* (phone calls), to *text* (email). Strategic decisions are usually bigger and more time consuming, whereas operational decisions are usually smaller and aim to create efficiencies for workers on a daily basis.

Chapter One: Capital Allocation

As we previously stated, *the financial services industry aims to assist individuals, corporations, and governments with capital allocation and maximizing capital efficiencies within any given business*. In this chapter, we will examine the principles of capital allocation.

To better understand capital allocation, please refer to the image below. It is a very simple image, but as we dive into the details of specific jobs, we will be magnifying various parts of this image.

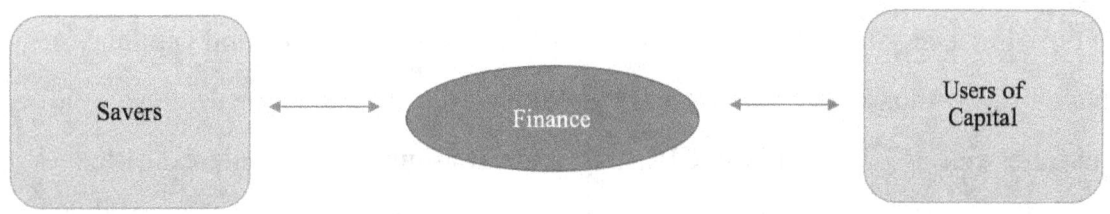

Figure One: Capital Allocation

From left to right, there are three major parties: 1) Savers, 2) Finance, and 3) Users of Capital.

Savers include individual savers, such as any person with a savings account, and collective savers, such as pension funds, insurance companies, sovereign wealth funds, and endowment foundations. Instead of allowing money to "sit" and depreciate in value[7], rational savers invest money through financial intermediaries and markets. The purpose of investing is to allow a gain to be

---

[7] Un-invested money depreciates in value over time due to inflation and opportunity cost.

realized on otherwise idle cash: your money "makes money" while just sitting around.

Users of capital include corporations, governments, and individuals. For example, if a family decides they want to become homeowners, usually the family will take out a mortgage from a bank to purchase a house because although they might have a suitable income to make payments on the loan, they do not have $300,000+ sitting around in cash for the purchase. Instead of purchasing it with all cash, they put $60,000 down, and borrow the rest. The bank charges interest on the loan—both parties win. The investor (the bank) makes interest on otherwise idle cash, and the borrower is able to purchase a home he or she did not have the cash to buy. Finance thus solves the mismatch of consumption needs and capital availability—those who have excess capital lend to those with needs they could not otherwise afford to satisfy. Charging interest aligns the self-interest of the capital provider with that of the capital user. For a very simple example, let us examine how capital allocation can theoretically assist an entrepreneur in launching a small business.

Connecting Savers with Users of Capital.

Capital allocation is a simple process to understand, and it is the primary function of a bank. Let's take the story of two individuals, Michael and Max, to show how finance mutually benefits both parties.

Michael is a wealthy individual who has more money than he can use for his own needs. Max is an entrepreneur with an idea for launching a deli shop (small business as distinct from a startup), but Max does not currently have enough money to launch his company. Michael and Max don't personally know each other and Michael and Max live several hundred miles apart from each other, but the two of these men can both mutually benefit from the use of a bank.

As stated earlier, Michael is wealthy and does not need all of the money he has, so he has elected to deposit a sum of $10,000 into a bank. Michael has elected to deposit this money into the bank because the bank pays interest, which means that Michael will make money just for depositing money into the bank. The bank tells Michael the following: "Michael, if you give us $10,000 today, your money will gain interest at the rate of 10% annually[8], so in one year from now, you'll have $11,000."

Max, who needs money to launch his business, goes to the bank to request a loan. The bank evaluates Max's business opportunity, and after careful consideration, the bank elects to write Max a loan. The bank tells Max the following: "Max, we will give you $10,000 today[9], conditioned on a 12% interest rate, so in one year from now you will give us back $11,200." Max is happy with the terms of the agreement, and is confident in his ability to spend the $10,000 now in starting his deli shop and have at least $11,200 to return in one year's time. In this situation, the bank makes $1,200, and everybody benefits.

Without the bank, it would be more difficult for borrowers and lenders to come into contact with one another, and even more difficult for an agreement to be reached between the two parties. By acting as a financial intermediary, the bank is able to make everybody happy.

Although this simple example explains the essence of the financial services industry, the reality is that capital allocation within the 21st century is much more

---

[8] For typical savings accounts, interest rates are currently less than 1% in the United States. We use 10% in this example because it's a simple calculation.
[9] Modern banks do not typically generate loans without collateral, but for the purposes of simplicity, we are going to pretend that Max does indeed qualify for a traditional bank loan.

complex. Specifically, modern day financiers like to divide financial firms into two categories: **sell-side**[10] and **buy-side**[11] firms.

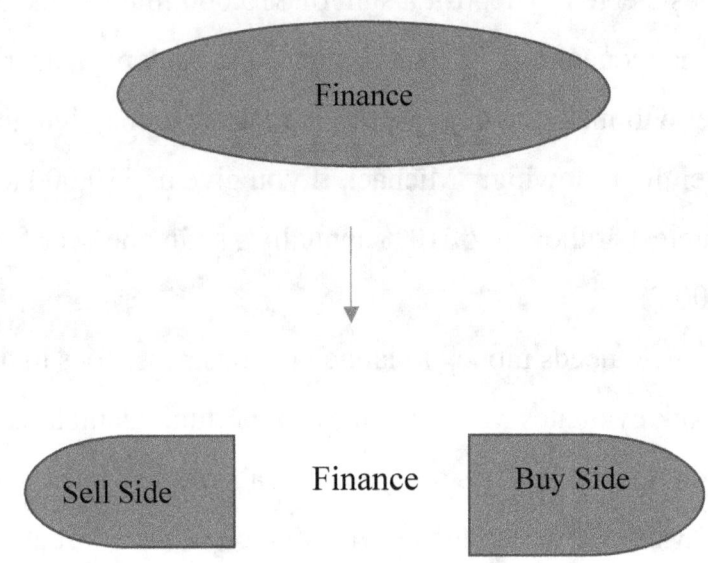

Figure Two: Division of Finance into Sell Side and Buy Side

Put simply, sell-side firms create and distribute a product, whereas buy-side firms purchase these products. The product, however, is not a product in the sense that a hover board, fidget spinner, or floral-patterned romper is a product. The products are generally securities or other instruments by which borrowers secure capital (i.e. financing) from lenders. The most straightforward example of why society needs investment banks involves the distribution of a new financial

---

[10] Sell-side firms include financial intermediaries, like investment banks, that focus primarily on selling financial securities.
[11] Buy-side firms include collective investors / savers that focus primarily on purchasing financial securities, like private equity firms, hedge funds, pension funds, etc.

product in the form of an IPO (initial public offering), which is the first instance in which a company allows its stock to be sold on a public exchange.

A Broad Overview of Sell-Side Finance through an IPO[12]

Background Story: Zoey is a recent graduate from an elite business school. Zoey is a bright woman. Before attending b-school, Zoey worked at a healthcare nonprofit that air-dropped measles vaccinations into remote tribal areas of Oceania and South America. Many decades ago, Western anthropologists visited these areas to document the relatively undisturbed cultures of the Earth's final frontiers. Unfortunately, the social scientists brought with them Western diseases, from which the natives had no immune defense. Of these diseases, measles became preventable through vaccination in the 1960s, but by the time the immunization had been developed, the tribes had become hostile to intruders as a result of their bringing disease. No longer able to enter into the forests of these tribes without fear of death by arrow shot, the anthropologists attempted to save the populations they almost destroyed by airdropping vaccinations in boxes into the forests where these tribes lived. In the boxes were immunization administration instructions written in the native tongue of the tribes. In test runs, the anthologists were horrified to see that when the boxes where dropped from the sky, the syringes within them broke upon the boxes' impact with the ground. Working quickly, they, along with a team of medical professionals, developed an oral vaccine half as effective as the syringe-administered vaccine, but capable of surviving fully intact the drop from the sky.

---

[12] A real-world example of an IPO is found in Appendix I.

The oral vaccine was a robust gel-like pill that could be dropped from thousands of feet in the air and still retain form when it hit the ground. With a hope and a prayer, the anthropologists began to drop boxes of these vaccines into the forests of Papua New Guinea and the deep Amazon. Miraculously, after ten years of these efforts, the populations of these tribes were observed by aerial photos to have doubled from the depths of the measles epidemic. It had been Zoey's job to oversee the continuing of these vaccination air drops along with expanding operations to a tribe that had been infected on the Sentinel Islands.

A Brilliant Idea: Having added value to society through her work at the non-profit, Zoey wished now to add value to her bank account by using the technology employed in the oral vaccines for other immunizations that American children normally undergo in their early years. She found that a sizeable number of people did not vaccinate their children due to the children's fear of needles, and that offering an oral (and watermelon-flavored!) alternative might bring her vast profits, while simultaneously helping American children. Teaming up with a group of biochemistry PhDs and marketing geniuses, she developed a product sound enough to secure venture capital financing[13]. Many sleepless nights and rounds of both equity and debt financings later, Zoey had grown her company into a **unicorn**[14].
 Wanting to 1) monetize that value for future growth and expansion and 2) seek a liquidity event for herself and her investors, Zoey and the venture capitalists sought an entrance to the public markets through an initial public offering (IPO). In an IPO, ownership is sold in the form of stock (or equity) to the public marketplace. For early investors and founders who retained ownership, this

---

[13] Venture capital (VC) financing is a form of private funding for startup companies. Venture capital is explained more in Part Three.
[14] A unicorn is a startup company with a multi-billion-dollar valuation.

personally means that the wealth they had stored in the company's valuation could now be unlocked by selling their stock. The company's stock allows its shareholders to possess 1) voting rights to the company and 2) residual cash flows generated by the company's operations. Zoey, who had an estimated net worth of $250 million on paper through her company's valuation, could eventually sell her equity stake after the IPO lock-up period expired and turn that on-paper number into cold, hard cash.

The Bank's Job: Zoey's vaccine company, DropPop, now hires an investment bank and begins the IPO process. The company negotiates how much equity will be sold for what price, and whether the investment bank will distribute the shares on a **firm commitment** or **best efforts basis**[15]. These negotiations go on within the **private side** of the bank, within the investment banking division[16]. The reason why we call this the private side of the bank is that this information MUST NOT LEAVE THE BANK and is of the highest confidentiality. If a banking analyst tries to be a **baller at the bar**[17] and impress the girl sitting next to him by talking about the deals he's staffed on in great detail, and anyone at the bank finds out, he is **100% likely to lose his job, his reputation, and his future**.

When the price for the shares is roughly agreed upon, the banker in the investment banking division will reach out to the banker in **equity capital**

---

[15] In a firm commitment basis transaction, the investment takes on the full risk of the securities it purchases for distribution to the public markets. In this case, the client is guaranteed a particular value for the sale of its securities. In a best efforts basis transaction, the investment bank sells the client's shares, but if shares remain unsold, is under no contractual obligation to purchase them.
[16] This is explained further in Part Two.
[17] For lack of a better term, we call this young, self-styled hotshot a (say it with emphasis) *finance douche*. He pronounces "finance" like "fin-ants" rather than "feye-nants" and probably has many deep insecurities about his self-worth. He goes to the bar and talks about the hours he works (which he inflates) like he is some type of superhero, when in reality, he is no more than an entry-level grunt ctrl-c-ing and ctrl-v-ing his way through long days and nights. Don't be this guy.

markets (ECM). Once the banker in ECM understands what kind of company is selling its equity, the ECM banker will talk to an **equity salesperson**. Not discussing specifics, the ECM banker will ask what passive institutional investors are currently looking at and what they are currently willing to buy. Having evaluated the market for the new shares, in a **firm commitment IPO,** the investment bank will purchase the shares (**underwrite**) at a set price, thus securing for DropPop a fixed sum of money. The investment bank will then sell the underwritten shares through equity salespeople who work on the public side of the bank (Markets / Securities / Sales & Trading).

These equity salespeople are the distribution channels through which the shares are sold and the **equity traders** (both humans and machines) provide secondary markets in the shares. If a buy-side account no longer wants to hold shares of the IPO, they can decide to sell them through an equity trader, who either buys them for position (**proprietary trading**) or crosses the shares to another investor (**market-making trading**). Through the secondary market, any retail investor can then purchase the shares of a company that had once been a young woman's metaphorical hobbyhorse. Through the many divisions of the investment bank, the ownership of DropPop has now been distributed and divided among many individuals and institutions who believe in the company's future, and all is right in the world.

The Dangers of Working in a Silo

Many who work within investment banks often become bogged down in the day-to-day activities and tasks associated with their individually narrow responsibilities. For those not involved in senior management, it is often easy to forget the "why" of what is being done versus the "how" of relatively complicated (but surprisingly unsophisticated) tasks. For that reason, it is essential to understand, even as an analyst, what functions the bank for which one works excels in. For example, it would not make sense to try hard for a job in a bank's M&A banking group, if it is eighth in the **league tables**[18] for that **product group**, and first for its oil and gas **industry group**[19].

Furthermore, if the bank is jettisoning senior people in unprofitable business divisions, it is always beneficial as a young employee to have friends in divisions within the bank that are expanding. If you are a young equity research associate with an interest in trading, and the bank is firing all the **equity research analysts**[20], it might be worth networking within the hypothetical bank's very profitable equities trading division for a potential transfer executed through internal mobility. Additionally, it is very unlikely anyone in a senior management role will be tolerated if they do not have a holistic view of how the bank functions in totality—if you want to rise to the top, it makes sense to understand everything going on more than superficially.

---

[18] League tables are provided by Bloomberg and rank banks by fees generated by groups within the investment bank.

[19] Product groups are generally mergers & acquisitions, leveraged finance, and restructuring, while industry groups focus on specific sectors like Natural Resources, TMT (tech, media & telecom), etc. This is explained more in Chapter Two.

[20] Senior professionals or managing directors within equity research are referred to as analysts, and their primary function is authoring reports on the publicly traded companies which they cover.

Part Two: Divisions of a Bulge Bracket Bank

Securities Division

Investment Banking Division	Fixed Income Sales & Trading	Equity Sales & Trading
Global Capital Markets		Equity Research
"Chinese Wall"	Asset Management	Private Wealth Management

Proprietary Trading

Private Bank

Part Two: Divisions of a Bulge Bracket Bank

All banks are slightly different, so there is no single, correct way to generalize the exact structure of a bulge bracket bank. We have included two images below, with the primary distinction being that the first image, from the Harvard Investment Association, shows a complete separation between the Investment Banking Division (IBD) and the Capital Markets or Global Capital Markets (GCM) Group, whereas the second image, shows a detailed outline of the IBD, with GCM being located within the IBD.

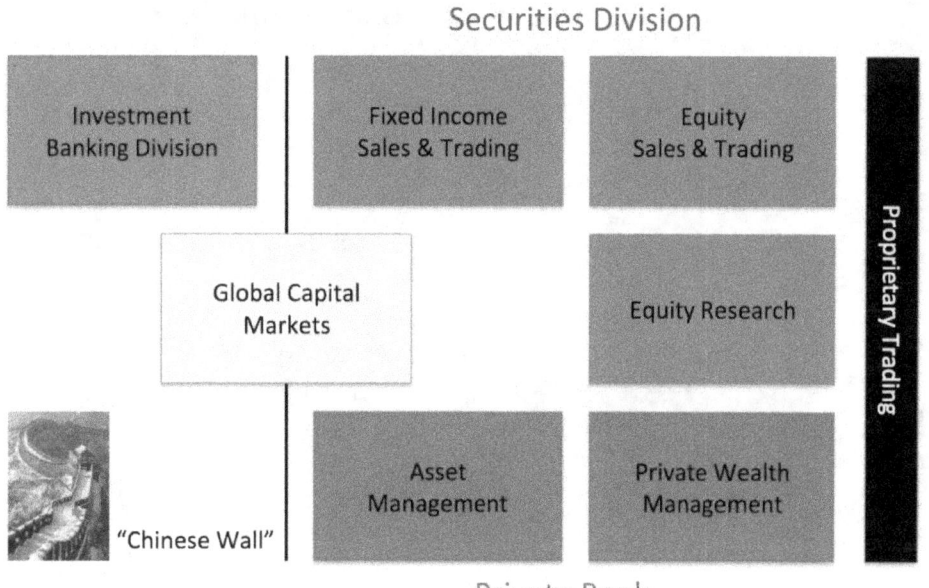

Figure Three: Bulge Bracket Bank Divisions

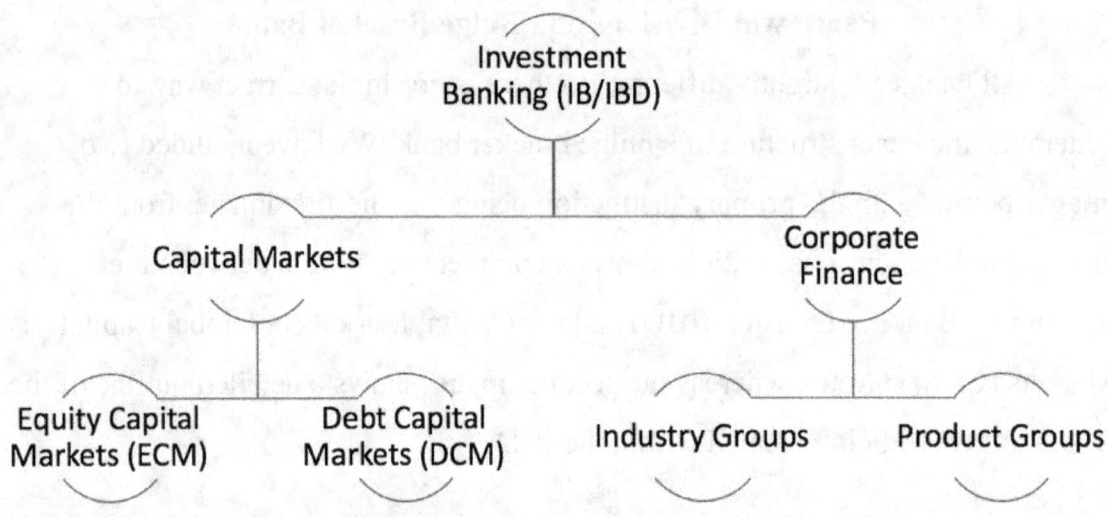

Figure Four: Divisions within IBD

Chapter Two: Investment Banking (IBD)

<u>What it is and Why it Matters</u>:

The investment banking division (IBD) is notoriously the most difficult entry-level sector in sell-side finance. The prestige of the job stems partly from the fact that investment bankers gain private information on their clients, usually public companies, in order to assist the clients in executing financial strategies. As a consequence of this insider information, investment bankers are not allowed to share the details of their day-to-day lives with anyone.

<u>The Business</u>:

The IBD of a bank makes money from the fees associated with providing advisory services on deals. For example, if an investment bank helps a company purchase another company, the total price of the acquisition may be $1B, and the bank takes a 5% cut of the total transaction ($50M). Bankers provide advisory services to businesses, help companies raise capital through underwriting equity and debt offerings, and help negotiate mergers and acquisitions (M&A).

<u>Key Firms</u>:

Just because someone works at an investment bank does not mean that he or she is technically an investment banker. Investment banks perform a variety of functions and offer a multitude of services, and the key front-office roles fall into Sales and Trading (S&T), Global Capital Markets (GCM), Equity Research (EQR), Private Banking (PB) and traditional investment banking services (corporate finance and / or M&A). Insiders at an investment bank are known to each other by the specific role which they perform: an equity trader will refer to himself as a trader, a research analyst will refer to herself as a research analyst, and the professional who works in mergers and acquisitions will call himself a banker. It is important to note that to industry outsiders, all these people may be referred to (incorrectly) as investment bankers. In actuality, only the person who works in the traditional IBD of the bank is truly an investment banker. Furthermore, true investment bankers refer to each other as "bankers" and not "investment bankers." The verbal distinction is superficially minute, but conveys an insider's knowledge.

For traditional investment banking (corporate finance and M&A), the biggest banks are known as "bulge brackets." In the United States, these are **Goldman Sachs**, **JP Morgan**, **Credit Suisse**, **Bank of America Merrill Lynch**, **Deutsche Bank**, **Citi**, **Barclays**, **Morgan Stanley**, and **UBS**. Some of these banks are headquartered outside the United States (Credit Suisse, Deutsche, Barclays, and UBS in particular), but maintain U.S. offices in New York City, the financial capital of the world. Additionally, some of these banks not only offer investment banking services, but are universal banks that also have commercial banking capabilities. Although you might have a checking account at the Bank of America down the block, the investment banking arm at BofA is far removed from this function.

Outside of the U.S., other big investment banks include **Nomura** (Japan), **Société Générale** (France), and **HSBC** (United Kingdom). These major investment banks are very large and hire mammoth analyst classes each year to fill many positions left open after the prior analyst classes get promoted to associate level, switch firms, switch careers, or go back to business school. As such, they tend to allocate many resources to recruiting, hiring, and training new analysts. On the other hand, there are thousands of **boutique and middle-market investment banks** throughout the United States, and first-year college graduates can also work here. Sometimes, these smaller banks offer larger salaries. Boutique investment banks, because they are smaller, cannot allocate the same resources to training new analyst classes and generally expect that new hires come prepared to work, having learned mostly everything about the job at a prior internship. Although there is less time, if any, devoted to training, working at a boutique can be very rewarding as a junior banker because more responsibility may be delegated to you. There may also be less bureaucracy and more direct facetime with senior bankers and managing directors, and this can be beneficial for those who dislike the corporate politics that are sometimes associated with bulge brackets.

A key distinction between boutique and bulge bracket banks is the relative levels of depth in the initial financial modeling done by analysts. Because bulge bracket banks have larger clients, models are needed more frequently to appease them, but the models need not be extremely in depth (if typed out on printer paper, this would be approximately 3-5 pages of modeling). Since boutique banks have smaller clients, models are needed less frequently and will receive more attention, so these models go more in depth (if typed out on printer paper, this would be approx. 18-26 pages).

Expected Pay:

Analysts at bulge brackets can expect a salary of $85,000 plus signing / relocation bonuses of $5,000-$20,000. Combined with the first-end-of-year bonus, first-year analysts can expect to make a total of anywhere from $100,000-

$185,000. Analysts at boutique banks can earn more or less, dependent on the quality of the bank.

Lifestyle and Hours:

Some people have referred to the banker lifestyle as the "bottles and models" career path. This is true, but the models look less like Kate Moss and more like Excel Spreadsheets. Junior bankers, primarily analysts, can expect to work six to seven days a week[21], fifty weeks of the year. Bankers work an average 80 to 120 hours a week, and have a schedule that is highly unpredictable. Banking is very client-centric, and as a result, the work can come in at any hour. Bankers typically arrive at the office between 9–10AM and, many days, do not work intensely until the afternoon. A client will typically contact the managing director (MD) with whom he has a relationship and ask that a certain task be done by the next morning. The work will fall down the chain of command until it hits the analyst's desk at about 5PM. It needs to be done by tomorrow morning—there are no excuses. The junior banker will work until the job is perfect, complete, and ready to be shown to the client. This might mean finishing it up by 10PM and going home before midnight, or it might mean being glued to the desk until the following morning. Either is fair game, but most nights, a banker can expect to be home by 2AM, but almost never before 8PM.

The work itself will primarily be building "pitch books." These are PowerPoint presentations that are comprised of financial models that are built using Excel. These pitch books give the client financial information that is relevant to the business of their firm or that of an acquisition target. Pitch books

---

[21] Some banks have begun to protect Saturdays for the health of their junior employees.

are presented to the clients by the senior bankers, so most of the time, the junior bankers have little to no facetime with clients. Since these pitch books will all be presented to clients, who are sometimes executives at Fortune 500 companies; every single detail must be correct, and thus, junior bankers quickly form a meticulous eye for detail.

There is no free lunch on Wall Street. First year bankers generally make more than their first-year brethren in S&T, GCM, and equity research, but they also definitely work the most. As an analyst moves up the ranks, the hours become more manageable, but many analysts only sign on for two or three years, after which they hope to use the valuable financial skill set they have learned to land a job in private equity or a financial role at a nonfinancial firm. The work is generally not very challenging from an academic / intellectual standpoint, but must be completed to perfection. Bankers have a steadfast eye for detail, and are often chewed out if they present a product that is not completely finished, with i's dotted and t's crossed. Luckily, the analyst position is temporary, and they will be able to leverage this transferable skill set to nearly every other career avenue if they decide to leave the industry.

Analyst Work:

For incoming analysts, there are two types of jobs in the investment banking division. The first type is a product group, and the second group is an industry group, which is also commonly called a coverage group.

If you work in a product group, you are spending every single day assisting senior bankers on a specific deal type across various industries, such as **M&A, Leveraged Finance, or Restructuring**. If you work in an industry / coverage group, you are spending every single day assisting senior bankers on a specific industry across various deal types, such as **Healthcare, Natural Resources, TMT (Technology, Media & Telecommunications), FIG (Financial Institutions Group), Industrials, Real Estate, etc.**

Product groups focus on mastering the valuation methods of their particular deal type, whereas coverage groups focus on mastering the specifics of their particular industry.

Exit Opportunities:

Professional financiers generally espouse the opinion that is no more transferrable and versatile skillset than that gained by the investment banker in his first two years on Wall Street. Having spent 100 hours a week for two years straight on grinding out pitch books and financial models, few 24-25-year-olds will have the same level of financial knowledge as do the graduates of Wall Street's boot camp. After two years as an analyst, a junior banker might stay at the bank as an associate, or jump ship for a position at a private equity firm. Some very talented individuals might join hedge funds, and still more will go on to get their MBAs. The two years a person spends as a junior banker are some of the toughest a person can endure in a career outside of military deployment. Accordingly, analysts who survive their two-year stints are often prized assets in any job market.

34

Chapter Three: Sales and Trading (S&T)

What it is and Why it Matters:

Sales and trading refers to the members of the bank that works in the public markets, as a part of the securities division (sometimes called the markets division) of a bulge bracket bank. Salespeople primarily sell financial securities (e.g. stocks and bonds) on the behalf of a client, whereas traders purchase and sell (trading) financial securities on behalf of the bank.

The Business:

Sales: Banks engage in securities market making in which they quote a bid and an ask price for a financial security. They (the market maker) sell at the higher (the ask) and buy at the lower (the bid) and make a spread (the difference) that compensates them for the risk of holding securities that may be negatively impacted by changes in the market price over time.

Trading: Banks engage in a limited amount of proprietary trading (commonly called "prop trading"), whereby the banks' traders take positions in securities with the goal of making a positive return. Prop trading was much more prominent before the 2008 Financial Crisis and the passage of the **Volcker Rule within the 2010 Dodd-Frank act**[22].

---

[22] The 2010 Dodd-Frank act was an act of Congress that introduced many new and stricter regulations governing Wall Street amid the fallout of the 2008 Financial Crisis. The Volcker Rule, which was a part of the legislation, was very punitive for the markets divisions of banks which had previously engaged in now prohibited proprietary trading activities.

Key Firms:

As with traditional investment banking, **Goldman Sachs, JP Morgan**, **Credit Suisse**, **Bank of America Merrill Lynch**, **Deutsche Bank**, **Citi**, **Barclays**, **Morgan Stanley**, **UBS**, and **HSBC** lead the pack for sales and trading. Since the legislation contained in Dodd-Frank came into effect, the Volcker Rule has placed constraining limits on banks' proprietary trading activity. Nowadays, the majority of trading that goes on at investment banks is market-making activity. If you are a born trader and want to take giant risk and trade for your own account, trading at an investment bank may be a great option, but you might want to look at the opportunities at hedge funds, such as **D.E. Shaw**, **Two Sigma**, and **Jane Street** if you have superior quantitative abilities.

Expected Pay:

Bulge brackets will pay a base salary of $85,000 and a signing bonus of $5,000-$20,000. End-of-year bonuses will typically bring the top analysts to $100,000 to $120,000 for the first year.

Lifestyle and Hours:

The day-to-day work of the trader and salesperson is quite different, but they both work around the same number of hours, with traders spending more time thinking of trade ideas and losing sleep over market movements, and salespeople spending evenings and weekends catering to clients (expensive dinners and rounds of golf, on the corporate card, of course).

The hours worked in the S&T division are generally determined by the hours in which the market is open. For most people, this means that their schedule is centered around the New York Stock Exchange (NYSE) hours of operation, but some people in the S&T division will work in foreign markets that operate in different time zones. In groups and products where trading occurs "over-the-counter," people generally work when their clients, or their counterparties[23], work—the hours are generally client-dictated.

Typically, traders and salespeople arrive at the office between 5:30 AM and 7:30AM, depending on their trading desk and market. Although the U.S. equity markets are open Monday through Friday 9:30 AM–4:00 PM[24], S&T professionals arrive before the markets open, and stay after they close. Typically, people work around 10 to 14 hours a day, and weekends are generally free for traders, while salespeople often spend at least one day of their weekend entertaining clients.

Although the hours worked are fewer than those in investment banking, the hours are often more intense, and tensions can run high during the closing hours of trading. Unlike in banking, where the primary source of revenue comes from fees associated with deals, revenue from trading comes from market-making in securities. If a trader buys a security that plummets in value, oftentimes he will need to dump it before the market closes in order to stop a greater loss from impacting the bank. Traders are given an enormous amount of responsibility because they are trading the bank's capital. If they lose enough and hide their losses[25], they can bankrupt the entire bank.

---

[23] Counterparties are the people on the other side of the trade – the person either selling a security to a trader or purchasing a security from a trader.

[24] Exceptions are made for US federal holidays, such as Christmas.

[25] To learn what not to do as a trader, read up on the story of Nick Leeson. http://www.nickleeson.com/biography/

Unlike banking, where there is a steep and strict ladder to the top, traders and salespeople are more quickly rewarded in the flatter hierarchy of trading desks. If traders make money for the bank, they can become managing directors by their late 20s. If salespeople bring on enough clients, then they can do the same almost as quickly. That said, if traders lose money and salespeople fail to bring on clients, they can quickly get the axe, and many do in fact get fired.

Additionally, there are many different products within sales and trading. Broadly speaking, trading desks are dichotomized into equities (stocks) and fixed income (bonds). Within these two large categories, the level of complexity of products traded varies widely. In particular, more complex products on the equities side consist of single-stock and index options (derivatives), whereas on the fixed income side, there are mortgage-backed securities (MBS) and credit-default swaps, amongst other credit products and credit derivatives. Currencies and commodities are often more closely related to the fixed income side, and individuals with a flair for mathematics and macroeconomics might find these areas interesting.

In short, sales and trading offers something for everyone in terms of markets; if you are at all interested in markets and macroeconomics and enjoy working in a team environment, this may be the role for you. Additionally, although traders may learn less transferable skills than do investment bankers, they become adroit in Bloomberg[26] and other trading technologies that enable them to become experts of their market.

Analyst Work:

---

[26] "Bloomberg" refers to Bloomberg Terminals, and for more info: https://en.wikipedia.org/wiki/Bloomberg_Terminal

The work of the sales analyst and trading analyst differs widely, but both must understand the products being sold to or traded with clients. The sales analyst will spend more time learning how to deal with accounts, and may be given some smaller accounts with which to build or enhance relationships, while the trading analyst will focus more time learning the product in depth and essentially serving as an apprentice to a senior trader. These days, a lot of what junior traders do is automating processes that their less tech-savvy superiors have to do manually. These tasks are not as flashy as the outside world presumes, and include pricing bespoke securities for clients, booking trades, flashing PNL[27], and determining the causes of various systems errors that undoubtedly occur. Sales analysts often have to schedule client events and are responsible for a lot of logistical planning of their senior salesperson's client-based outings. Banks, even today, have subpar technology when compared to their buy-side clients, so the job of trading analysts is often more frustrating on a technical level than the job of junior salesperson. That said, junior traders might have to deal with fewer offensive or egotistical personalities than do junior salespeople. In the opinion of someone who worked as a junior trader, I would recommend any who go down this path to have an established technical background with knowledge of basic economics, computer programming in Visual Basic or Python, and an aptitude for working under extremely tight deadlines. In the frenzy of the trading day, more than anything, junior traders and salespeople need to be able to take harsh criticism and insults on the chin, and be able to react quickly to new situations. No matter how hard the

---

[27] Flashing PNL refers to the junior analyst's job of computing how much his senior trader(s) has / have made or lost that day. In liquid securities, this is a relatively quick task; with more illiquid instruments, this can take several hours.

day is, most desks will let you go home by 7:00PM to de-stress (with the exception of client outings, which can last long into the night).

Exit Opportunities:

The skill set learned in sales can be applied to any other sales position (such as fundraising for a hedge fund, private equity fund, or a venture capital fund), but overall, the skillset is less marketable than that learned in the traditional IBD. Some salespeople, if they grow tired of the rough-and-tumble of the trading floor, go back to business school.

Traders are the experts of the markets and products they trade. Generally, if they are good at their jobs and make money for the bank, they tend to stay and move up the ranks on their trading desk. Unlike banking, where you work in a bullpen in relative silence, traders are constantly involved in conversation about taking and exiting positions. For those who thrive in this busy and lively environment, there is little else that would satisfy them for a career. As a result, for those who are successful trading analysts, there is less turnover than in an investment banking analyst classes, where almost all junior bankers jump ship after two years. Successful traders will either move up the ranks on their desk, join trading desks at other banks, move to hedge funds to trade there, or, in the case where they want to do something else in the financial sector aside from trading, go back to business school. The skill set acquired by trading analysts is less transferable than that of a banker. Generally, professionals in other areas of finance look favorably upon traders who have successfully and consistently beaten the market, and who want to explore other areas of finance. Although less common than in banking, there are cases of younger traders leveraging connections to secure positions at private equity and venture capital firms, without having to attend business school.

Chapter Four: Global Capital Markets (GCM)

What it is and Why it Matters:

Global Capital Markets refers to the division of the bank that connects the investment banking division with the securities division. For example, investment bankers usually work privately with clients to create a product, such as a corporate bond. The global capital markets division is responsible for overseeing the sale of this product to the public markets. Whereas the IBD deals exclusively in private information, GCM operates with both private and public information. Due to the sensitivity of holding private information right before it becomes public information, those working in Global Capital Markets are required to be very cautious in discussing information with other bankers. Only when GCM steps out to the trading floor to present the new issue to equity salespeople (with every i dotted and t crossed) has the information become public.

The Business:

The GCM group of most investment banks can be divided into two main parts: equities capital markets (ECM) and debt capital markets (DCM). The ECM group works closely with those in the IBD on Initial Public Offerings (IPOs), Seasoned / Secondary Equity Offerings (SEO), Private Investment in a Public Equity (PIPE), or Convertible Securities. The DCM Group is usually compartmentalized into various product groups, which can include Global

Structured Credit Derivatives, Global Structured Credit Products, Domestic Liabilities Management, Financial Institutions, and Asset-Backed Finance Group.

In short, the IBD helps clients create a product. The S&T Division sells the product. The GCM Division is the middleman who helps the client decide when and how to sell the product.

Key Firms:

Essentially all the bulge brackets.

Lifestyle and Hours:

Analysts do work that is essentially between banking and sales and trading. Naturally, their hours tend to be somewhat market-structured, and range between S&T hours and IBD hours. Analysts can expect to work from 8:00 AM–9:00 PM five days a week, and generally will come to the office one day a weekend for a few hours to catch up on work.

Expected Pay:

Bulge brackets will pay a base salary of $85,000 and a signing bonus of $5,000-$20,000. End-of-year bonuses will typically bring the top analysts to $100,000 to $120,000 for the first year.

Analyst Work:

Analysts are responsible for knowing their market intimately. Occasionally analysts will formulate reports on recent trading patterns within the market and historical analysis, and might also be involved in preparing investor presentations for **roadshows**[28]. Because GCM members will be dealing with not only the client and investors, but also everyone responsible to those two parties at the bank, strong interpersonal skills are a must-have.

Exit Opportunities:

We believe that the GCM is not the best place to start out in the bank if a private equity or hedge fund job is the end goal. On the other hand, GCM is generally a good fit for someone who likes the work and wants to move up the corporate ladder within that department. GCM analysts are not PE firms' first choice for recruiting, nor are they HFs first choice for trading / research recruiting. Personally, I have found people who have gone into this division right out of school do not want to do IBD, found the work interesting, wanted a name on their resume, but did not necessarily want to stay in finance.

---

[28] In a roadshow, the bank presents new issue stocks or bonds to potential institutional buyers.

Chapter Five: Private Bank (Private Wealth Management & Asset Management)

What it is and Why it matters:

The private bank division of a bulge bracket bank refers to the sector of the bank that is responsible for handling other people's investments and caters to wealthy individuals, families, and endowments. Specifically, the asset management group is responsible for investing the money of clients who are usually institutional investors such as pension funds, insurance companies, or corporations. The private wealth management (PWM) group is responsible for investing the money of clients, who are almost always high net worth (HNW) or ultra high net worth (UHNW) individuals. Unlike a hedge fund, the private bank usually has a less aggressive investment philosophy, in which securities are not frequently bought or traded. Most investments made by the private bank are long-term security purchases. Additionally, most ultra high net worth and high net worth individuals differ from the retail buyer of stocks—these people are not interested in Pink Sheet, Small Cap stocks which might have the potential to skyrocket. They are already rich, and primarily are interested in diversifying and preserving their wealth.

The Business:

Private banking, both private wealth management and asset management, are highly centered around satisfying clients' needs. Unlike in IBD, jobs in private banking are buy-side opportunities. Analysts will be assisting in the creation of unique portfolios for individual clients, and the security purchases of these portfolios are generally long-term positions. In the IBD, the overall goal is to sell financial strategies that will generate a fee for the bank, but in private banking, the overall goal is to onboard as many clients as possible. This is because there is a management fee associated with the total amount of assets a client holds with the private bank.

Generally, private bankers with a large number of clients on the higher end of the wealth spectrum ($10-25 million net worth) will get paid more than entry-level bankers who only handle accounts which scrape the minimum requirements ($250-500K net worth). Private bankers with ultra high net worth clients usually need to be more sophisticated because the concerns of the super rich are often more nuanced than those of lower net worth clients . For the very wealthy, primary concerns include 1) estate planning 2) wealth preservation 3) generating low-risk income and 4) reducing tax obligations. In terms of estate planning, good private bankers know their clients' needs well and will be able to suggest and explain products that will enable wealthy individuals to pass on their wealth without significant impacts due to estate taxes and other death-related fees. A good private banker knows the current regulatory environment and recent tax legislation and will be able to steer his clients to products that junior private bankers might not even know exist. Wealth preservation may involve hedging a client's business risks by constructing a portfolio that complements their income source (e.g. if the client owns a luxury car dealership, investing in counter-cyclical stocks might ensure the financial safety of the client). Generating low risk income is especially important for retirees who have amassed wealth during their professional lives, and now want to enjoy their wealth without depleting it from future generations.

Reducing tax obligations may require knowing tax-advantaged securities, like municipal bonds, to a T, such that the banker can explain how using them in a portfolio can generate a tax-friendly yield to an income-hungry client. No matter what, an emphasis on client relationships and interpersonal skills is crucial to ensure that the client stays with the bank and that when the client has a need, the private banker knows best how to service it.

Key Firms:

Morgan Stanley, Goldman Sachs Asset Management (GSAM), Credit Suisse Asset Management (CSAM), UBS, and JP Morgan.

Expected Pay:

$55,000 – $100,000.

Lifestyle and Hours:

The lifestyle and hours are generally more relaxed than the hours associated with other divisions of bulge bracket banks. Most analysts work 40-50 hours a week. Initially, there may be a large emphasis on adding new clients to the digital rolodex if you start out in private wealth management.

<u>Analyst Work</u>:

In the PB division, the two main roles are investment professionals and relationship managers. The investment professionals are responsible for analyzing portfolios and recommending new products to be purchased by clients, whereas the relationship managers are responsible for maintaining the relationship with the clients and selling the products recommended by the investment professionals. Most analysts can be expected to fulfill the role of the investment professional.

<u>Exit Opportunities</u>:

Private wealth management and asset management are often the exit opportunities from other jobs. That said, it is not unheard of for relationship managers to become investor relations professionals for buy-side firms, and some investment professionals in PWM can go on to work for family offices[29].

---

[29] Family offices serve an individual (or potentially a few) extremely wealthy family(ies). The services rendered by the family office often go beyond what is expected of private bankers.

Chapter Six: Equity Research (EQR)

What it is and Why it matters:

The equity research division of a bulge bracket bank is responsible for analyzing a group of stocks for the purposes of formulating research reports that grade the stocks on a buy, sell, or hold basis. These reports are generally used by the firm's internal S&T division, institutional investors, and other buy-side firms (such as mutual funds or hedge funds).

The Business:

The equity research division places an emphasis on mastering a small group of stocks (5-15). Analysts are usually placed into a coverage / industry group, and quickly become experts in their field. Analysts are responsible for maintaining comprehensive detailed financial models of their covered companies, writing the reports of their covered companies, and frequently communicating with the management teams of their covered companies. Most notably, analysts must be able to quickly respond to new information about their companies, and the releasing of quarterly earnings reports usually marks the beginning of a few long days in which the analysts must stay late to dissect the information and formulate an updated report on their companies.

Key Firms:

JP Morgan, Goldman Sachs, Credit Suisse, Citi, Morgan Stanley, UBS, Bank of America Merrill Lynch[30].

Expected Pay:

$85K, bonus can be anywhere from $0-20K.

Lifestyle and Hours:

Junior people in equity research will generally work a bit more than market hours most of the year (70 hours a week), but during earnings season, they work well into the night figuring out how quarterly financial statements should impact their target prices for the companies they cover. Weekends are generally pretty free, but the intensity of the work will largely depend on how committed the senior analyst is to publishing new and worthwhile research reports.

Analyst Work:

Equity research associates generally learn a good deal about modeling public companies, and may help senior analysts in preparing marketing material and communicating new price targets to the internal sales and trading team.

---

[30] Pretty much all the bulge brackets care about equity research because it can be given to institutional clients to entice trading, which in turn generates market-making commissions for the bank.

<u>Exit Opportunities</u>:

The best equity research associates should hope to jump ship to buy-side roles in fundamental equities hedge funds. At these funds, the research performed does not have the positive, buy-rating skew that is found in sell-side research reports[31].

---

[31] Sell-side research tends to be more positively biased because the bank makes money when corporations engage the investment banking division as an advisor. Because of this, equity research analysts are often reluctant to put a sell rating on any firm that the bank currently retains as an investment banking client. Doing this would be like a beautician telling a client's friends that she was ugly without her makeup on—not a wise business decision.

Chapter Seven: Popular Exit Opportunities (HF, PE, VC)

Note: Part Three is exclusively focused on an introductory explanation of venture capital and private equity, whereas this final chapter in Part Two discusses some of the employment opportunities following a stint in banking.

<u>What it is and why it matters:</u>

Once you have graduated from an analyst program at a bulge bracket bank, you will soon find yourself up against bonus ceilings. If you are a very talented undergraduate or someone who has been in industry for a few years, chances are, you will want to maximize potential compensation and seek a job on the buy side, specifically at a hedge fund (HF), private equity (PE) firm, or venture capital (VC) firm. If you are lucky enough to land one, you will be expected to perform right out of the box, but can be paid many times the average salaries offered by sell-side institutions. These jobs are the most highly sought after in finance, and if you think you are at the top of the field, they may be just right for you.

<u>The Business:</u>

Hedge funds (HF) have differing mandates, but all seek to generate positive absolute returns on their assets under management, or AUM. Generally, hedge funds are compensated with 2% of AUM and 20% of all profits.

Private equity (PE) firms seek to buy distressed or underperforming businesses by engaging in leveraged buyouts. After purchasing these companies, PE firms either restore them to profitability by correcting operational issues and financial problems that had existed under previous ownership, or expand the business to increase its total valuation. If successful, PE firms cash in when they take the company public in an IPO or resell it to another private market buyer[32].

Venture capital (VC) firms buy equity stakes in startups with the intention of providing advice and guidance to grow the small businesses quickly, and because the VC firm purchases an equity stake early on, the value of the startup equity has the potential to increase exponentially. The ultimate goal for a VC is a successful exit that is characterized by a liquidity event, wherein the startup goes public in an IPO or is bought by another company.

Key Firms:

The biggest and most prestigious hedge funds are **Bridgewater Associates** (global macro), **Point72 Asset Management** (long / short equity), **Baupost Group** (long / short equity), **AQR** (diversified), **Och-Ziff Capital Management** (diversified), **Jane Street** (quantitative), **D.E. Shaw** (quantitative), and **Renaissance Technologies** (quantitative). Big players within the PE space are **KKR**, **Blackstone**, **TPG**, and **The Carlyle Group**, and major VC firms include **Kleiner Perkins Caufield & Byers**, **Sequoia**, and **Bessemer Venture Partners**. It is important to note that these firms hire very few individuals straight out of college, and some firms (in particular, Renaissance Technologies) hire virtually no one straight out of college. That said, despair not, because if you are at the top of your elite college class and have had prior experience in finance, a job at some of these firms can still be on your application radar.

---

[32] PE firms can also cash in when the purchased company becomes profitable. As the primary or sole owner of the company, PE firms can receive a portion of the company's profit in the form of dividends.

Expected Pay:

If you work in the front office at any of these firms, it is highly unlikely you will make less than $100,000 your first year out of undergrad. Many of these firms are very secretive to the outside world about their compensation structure, but talented individuals have been known to make upwards of $250,000 in total pay for their first year.

Lifestyle and Hours:

Hedge Funds: At some quantitative firms, traders can work around market hours and generally work between 60 and 70 hours a week. At other firms, particularly long / short equity firms, where analysts perform valuation modeling on companies much like the valuation modeling performed by investment bankers, first-years can expect to work 60 to 80 hours a week, but at some of the most cutthroat funds, this number can be just as high as it is in investment banking. It really all depends on where you work and the culture at each firm because any two hedge funds are more different compared to each other than any two bulge bracket investment banks are to each other. No matter what, you will work long and hard in order to generate positive returns in any market. Hedge funds are notoriously competitive, with an intense focus on the bottom line.

Private Equity: At some firms (Blackstone in particular), many analysts are hired right out of undergrad. As an industry insider, I can attest to the fact that the hours worked by first-year analysts at the larger PE firms are the most grueling in finance. A particularly hard-working and talented analyst worked 140 hours one week, and another worked 16-20 hours days for a month straight, reaching a point at which she had to be admitted to the hospital because of health issues.

That said, most smaller PE firms and those without large analyst classes can expect first-years to work between 60 to 80 hours a week. Generally, the hours are more manageable than investment banking because PE firms are the clients to whom investment banks cater.

Venture Capital: Venture capital is notoriously hard to break into straight out of college. VC firms are typically very small and only hire people with one or more of (1) an insider's knowledge of a particular technical field relevant to the startups the VC backs (2) prior experience as an entrepreneur at a successful startup (3) investment banking experience and vast expertise in financial modeling and people skills, or (4) a near-endless rolodex of contacts in the industry in which the VC is a leader. Venture capitalists generally need to be financially savvy, but most of their work is comprised of sorting through many startups and picking the wheat from the chaff. This is a difficult task relying heavily on past experience and intuition; when a startup has no revenue, any financial modeling that could be done would be guesswork at best. After sourcing ventures to back, the task of assisting the entrepreneurs to grow their business quickly becomes paramount. The hours worked at VCs can vary widely, but venture capitalists generally work between 60 to 80 hours a week.

Exit Opportunities:

In short, these buy-side jobs are the exit opportunities of other jobs. Many people work years in investment banking in order to secure positions at these firms, so generally the main exit opportunities are within other firms in the same industry. For venture capitalists, becoming a successful entrepreneur is an option, but for the most part, few people who have these prestigious and high-paying jobs want to quit and risk ending up with nothing. For those with only a few years under their belts, business school might still be an option, but generally if you can land a position at a top hedge hund, PE firm, or VC, you should stay within the space, move up the ranks, and become the next master of the universe.

Part Two Summary

- Bulge Bracket Banks operate with both private and public information.

- The Investment Banking Division (IBD) of a bank works primarily on the private side of the financial markets. Investment bankers help a company *make* a financial product (e.g. stock offering, debt offering).

- The Sales & Trading (S&T) Department of a bank works exclusively on the public side of financial markets.

- The Global Capital Markets (GCM) Division of a bank works on *both* the private and public sides of financial markets. The GCM Division is responsible for overseeing the sale of the products made by investment bankers.

- The Private Bank (Wealth Management & Asset Management) Division of a bank works with clients on managing the investments and elements of diversification in a client's portfolio.

- The Equity Research Division of a bank produces regular reports on companies, with an investment rating of either Buy, Sell, or Hold.

- The Buy-side Exit Opportunities are attractive for many reasons, particularly 1) pay 2) prestige and 3) lifestyle.

Part Three: Intro to Venture Capital and Private Equity

Figure Five: The Valley

Part Three: Intro to Venture Capital and Private Equity

Before diving into various types of careers in private financial markets, I would like to clarify the role of the private investor.

Most of the time, private businesses are relatively small, and therefore are not listed on a public stock exchange. These businesses usually welcome additional capital for the purposes of growth: money can act as a fuel for growing businesses. Sometimes, these businesses do not qualify for traditional bank loans. Perhaps the business is a technology startup, with no assets, and therefore, nothing that the bank can collateralize. Since debt cannot be used to fuel the growth of the startup, the startup seeks an equity investment from a private investor. A rational private investor is incentivized to make an investment in a private business if the opportunity can provide financial returns that are higher than the returns associated with investments on public stock exchanges. Inherently, there is an increased amount of risk for an investment in a private business when compared to an investment in a public company, but savvy private investors can factor in the appropriate amount of risk for the specific opportunity into the criteria surrounding their investment decision.

In exchange for his capital, the private investor usually receives shares (stock) in the private business. This stock can generate money (a return on the investment) through two avenues:

1) Dividends: a distribution of a company's earnings to shareholders.
2) Capital Gains: a profit from selling the shares in the future when the stock's value increases.

Although dividends can be a steady source of income, professional private investors usually seek to generate a return on investment (ROI) through capital gains.

Professional Private Investors – The Current Market (2018)

Most professional private investors raise a fund for the sole purpose of making private investments (E.g. venture capital and private equity funds). These funds are raised from the money provided by a variety of people / institutions, and the people / institutions providing the capital are called **limited partners**. The limited partners legally commit to provide a sum of money to the fund when called upon for the length of the fund's lifecycle, which is usually a ten-year period. The fund uses this money to make investments. The fund generates a return through capital gains (buying a stock for a low price and then selling it for a higher price). If successful, the fund returns the original principal investment to the limited partners, while also, 80% of the profits generated are also given to the limited partners. The fund, for generating successful returns, gets to keep 20% of the profits[33].

There are, of course, some caveats to the description I have laid out. First and foremost, the fund lifecycle is not always fixed as ten years, but this is the most common lifecycle length seen throughout the industry. This description also did not take into management fees: most venture capital and private equity funds

---

[33] Sometimes this breakdown isn't at 80 / 20. It depends on the specific firm– successful firms can sometimes require more profit to be shared since the investment has been historically "safe", whereas new firms could incentivize limited partners to invest be agreeing to return a larger share of the profits (e.g. 90 / 10 split).

charge their investors a fee for managing the total amount of money. This fee is usually around 1-2% of the total assets under management (AUM), and is used to cover fixed expenses, such as salaries, office space, travel expenses, etc. Although large funds do generate a steady amount of income from management fees, ideally, the fund is successful and the real money to be made is in the profit sharing mechanism.

The most attractive careers in private financial markets fall into two different categories:

1) Venture Capital (VC)
2) Private Equity (PE)

For the most part, **venture capital** aims to invest money into early-stage businesses (startups), and **private equity** aims to invest money into later-stage businesses. Venture capital usually takes a minority stake (less than 50% ownership) in a new business, whereas private equity usually seeks a majority stake (more than 51% ownership) in a mature business that has a history of producing steady cash flows by utilizing an established business model.

Before I proceed further, I would like to define private equity in a manner that reflects best practices in the financial services industry, which is how I will be using the phrase. The standard dictionary definition for private equity is as follows: "private equity is capital that is not noted on a public exchange."[34] The problem with this broad, dictionary definition is that it does not differentiate

---

[34] Please see the following link for the definition:
http://www.investopedia.com/terms/p/privateequity.asp.

venture capital firms from private equity firms, although I have clearly stated stark differences between the two practices. Practitioners more commonly use the phrase "private equity" when referring to firms that frequently use a leveraged buyout (LBO) model, an acquisition strategy that collateralizes the assets of the target company. Practitioners almost exclusively use the phrase "venture capital" when referring to firms that exclusively make investments in startup businesses.

In recent times, there have been many different crossovers between venture capital and private equity. To best describe these crossovers, it may be useful to examine the role of **growth equity**. Growth equity is a form of capital deployed into relatively mature businesses for expansion purposes. Growth equity can come from either venture capital or private equity firms, depending on the specific business in question. There are relatively few Firms that exclusively focus on growth equity, but one notable example is **General Atlantic**, located in New York City.

Chapter Eight: Venture Capital

Venture capital is a form of a private investment in risky, relatively new, startup companies. Venture capital usually takes the form of a minority equity investment, meaning that the venture investor does not seek absolute control of the invested company.

<u>Background Information:</u>

Venture capital is inherently risky, since the entire idea is to invest in companies when there is little-to-no proof of business concept. Companies that seek venture capital are aiming to use the money for the purposes of rapid growth. Money can be used for hiring additional talent and marketing, which can help the company grow more quickly than without money. Sometimes, products require large sums of money, for development purposes, before paying off, so many venture-backed companies are not profitable for several years. The attractive feature of startup companies is that once profitability is achieved, it usually can also grow exponentially. This makes ownership in the company very valuable if it is exhibiting potential for exponential profit growth. Therefore, venture investors seek to make investments when the company is young, and usually not profitable, so that the investor's ownership stake (equity / stock) can be sold at a later date for more money than when it was purchased.

Before Moving Forward: An important note is to be said about startup companies. Although the dream of being the next Facebook or Amazon is appealing to entrepreneurs, the reality is that most startup companies will never raise venture capital – most companies fail before receiving any kind of institutional financing. For the companies that do end up raising capital, most of these companies also fail. A company can fail for a number of reasons, and at any point in the fundraising process, a company can simply fail and not move on to the next round of financing. In the case of failure, investors usually seek to force the company into a sale so that some money, but perhaps not all of the principal investment, can be returned. Sometimes, nobody wants to buy the company. In this case, the investor usually loses all invested capital[35].

There are a number of different models and stages of investing within the venture capital space. For the purpose of simplicity, I would like to first examine traditional venture capital as broken into two groups: early-stage venture investors and later-stage venture investors. Both of these groups of investors seek to make private investments that will provide returns well above the opportunities available in public markets, the main difference being in the risk / return balance.

---

[35] Some startups don't fail and don't succeed, and this is seen when a company stops growing but is profitable. Most of the time, if a sale cannot be achieved, the company will perform a stock buyback, so that investors can exit the company.

Venture Type	Hold Period	% 0-1X ROI (Failure)	% 1-5X ROI	% 5-10X ROI	% 10-20X ROI	% 20-50X ROI	% 50X+ ROI (Home Run)
Early-Stage	8 Years	64.8	25.5	5.9	2.5	1.1	0.4
Late-Stage	6 Years	29	57	14	N/A	N/A	N/A

Figure Six: ROI[36]

How it Works:

Early-stage venture investors invest in Seed-Stage, Series A, and Series B rounds of funding of a startup company.

- Seed-Stage is generally the first round of institutional funding that a startup receives. Not all startup companies seek a **seed-stage round of financing**: some companies forgo the opportunity for Seed Capital, and instead, try to make Series A the first institutional round of funding. Investments at this stage typically range from $1M – $3M[37], and usually, a team of founders has been established, there is an initial business plan, and in the case of a

---

[36]Data has been provided by the following website:
http://www.industryventures.com/2017/02/07/the-venture-capital-risk-and-return-matrix/.
[37] The valuation of the company is highly dependent on a number of qualitative factors, such as previous entrepreneurial experience, market size, and risk of investment. As a rule of thumb, venture investors usually seek a 15–33% stake in the company at each round of funding.

technology company, a Minimum Viable Product (MVP) [38] has been created.

- Series A is the first "big" round of funding for most companies. Investments at this stage typically range from $3M – $12M, and usually, the company has established executive roles between the founders, the company has hired employees, the product has hit market, and there has been exponential growth in either a) number of users / clients, or b) revenue. Companies are typically not profitable at this stage.

- Series B is the last "early-stage" round of venture financing. Investments at this stage can range from $5M – $30M, all dependent on how the company has performed since its latest round of financing.

For these early rounds of financing, there are three major points to expand upon:

1) Time Between Rounds: Startups, if successful, usually close a new round of funding every 12 – 18 months. If the company is beginning to takeoff and money is being burned more quickly than originally planned, many investors would be happy to start a new round of funding even earlier. If the company is performing poorly, investors may be hesitant to further fund the company, and an additional round of capital could take longer than 18 months (or never occur at all).

2) Dilution: Every company begins with a fixed number of shares of stock. As a company accepts funding, the company issues new shares of stock, thus, diluting total ownership of previous investors. Although previous investors

---

[38] A Minimum Viable Product is a development technique in which the technology has been created to an adequate means for early adopters, but is not yet ready to launch for the full market.

own less of a percentage of the company in a new round of funding, the value of their shares increases significantly, so they are still making money[39].

3) Valuation: in addition to valuation being dependent on a number of qualitative factors within the individual startup, valuations also fluctuate according to macroeconomic conditions. The below charts outline the difference in valuations between 2010 and 2014. Although the startups that were funded in 2014 were *probably* not more valuable than the startups funded in 2010, there is a substantial increase in mean / median valuations[40].

4) Exit Opportunities (How People Make Money): As stated early, most professional private investors seek to generate a return on the investment through capital gains. Capital gains are achieved through a liquidity event. A liquidity event is an instance in which a company's shares are exchanged for cash, ideally at a higher value than when they were purchased. The most common examples of a liquidity event are an acquisition or Initial Public Offering (IPO). In a liquidity event, all shareholders trade their shares in for cash, which means that the entrepreneur, who may have put in little-to-no capital when starting the company, and investors "exit" the investment.

---

[39] An exception to this rule would be if a company accepts a "down round" of funding, a fundraising round in which the total company value decreases from the previous round. Down rounds are generally not good, but sometimes necessary for the purposes of survival.
[40] Source for : https://pitchbook.com/news/articles/the-series-a-b-c-valuation-distribution-for-us-companies-is-moving

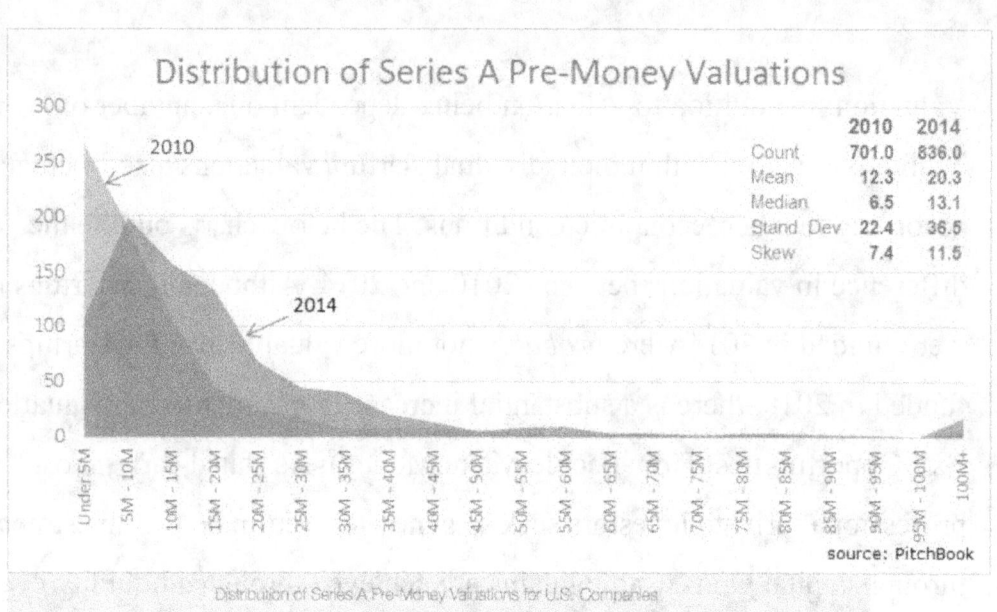

Figure Seven: Series A

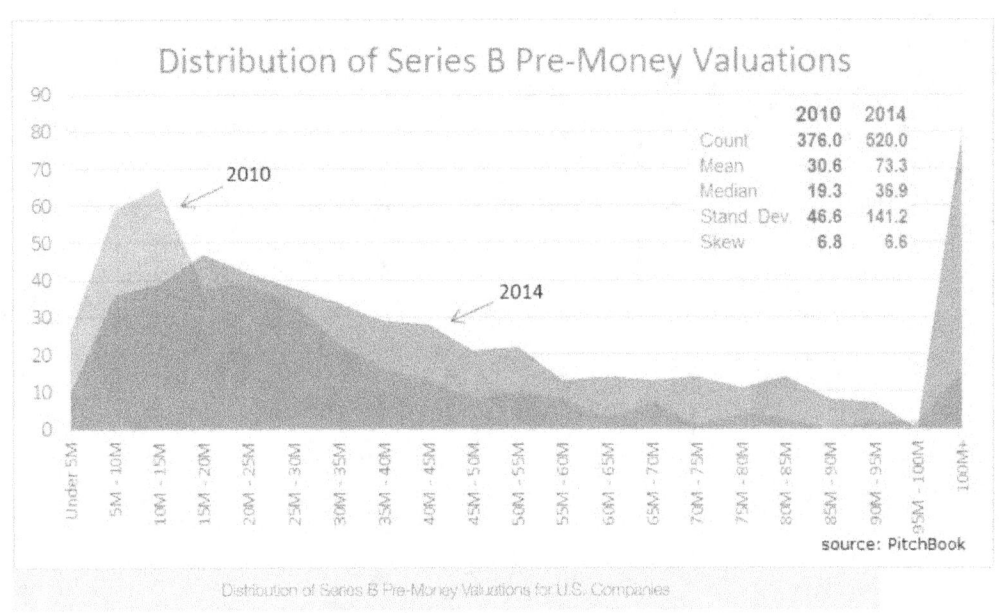

Figure Eight: Series B

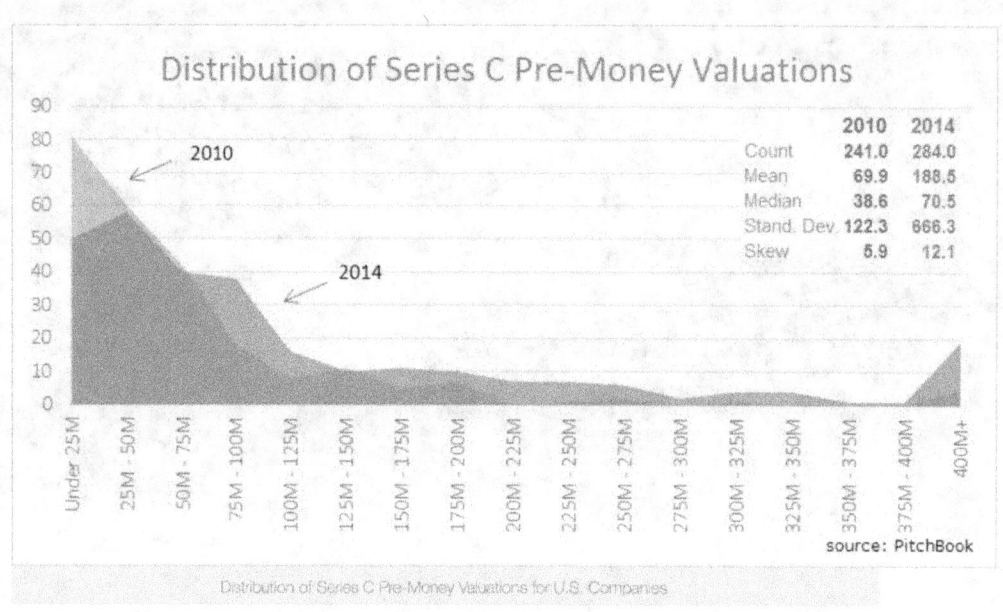

Figure Nine: Series C

Late-stage venture investors invest in Series C, Series D, and beyond rounds of funding of a startup company. Later-stage venture capital may also be referred to as growth equity. This is a very interesting stage of funding, because as seen in the chart above, the average Series C valuation of these companies more than *doubled* between 2010 and 2014.

Chapter Nine: Private Equity

Private equity is a form of private investment in businesses with a low risk profile. Private equity investments are most commonly characterized as investments in stable or more mature investments, but within the last decade, private equity has expanded to include investments in more risky, smaller companies from time-to-time. Private equity usually takes the form of a majority buyout, meaning that the private equity investor seeks absolute control of the invested company, by purchasing a majority, if not all, of the shares of stock.

Background Info:

Private equity is inherently less risky than venture capital, since the businesses that are targeted for investments have been established and generate steady cash flows. Usually, private equity investors seek out businesses to buy, but sometimes, business owners / managers may seek the help of private equity investors for the purposes of expansion or restructuring the ownership of the business. There are two major kinds of markets in the private equity industry: **middle market PE Firms** and **mega fund PE** Firms.

- Middle Market Private Equity Firms seek to invest in firms that are not extremely small but are also not large, publically traded companies: as the name may suggest, these private equity firms are seeking to invest in companies that are in the middle of their respective markets. The annual revenues of a middle market company can range from $10M – $1B.

- Mega Fund PE Firms seek to invest in large companies, which are sometimes publically traded. If the company is publically traded, the PE firm will be taking the company "private", which means it will remove the company from the public stock exchange by making a tender offer[41] to a majority, or all, of the current shareholders.

All kinds of private equity firms use leverage in the majority of their investments.

How it Works:

A leveraged buyout is the acquisition of another company using a significant portion of debt (very similar to a mortgage). For example, let's pretend I'm buying a business that operates as a factory. I go to the owners of the business and ask how much money they want, they tell me $100M. The problem is that I only have $10M in my pocket, so I decide to use debt to finance the other $90M. First, I go to a couple banks to figure out what can be marked as collateral, and the banks agree that the factory's parts (real estate, equipment, etc.) could be easily marked as collateral for $80M[42]. Now that I have a total of $90M, I need just another $10M in debt. Since there's not much else that can be marked as collateral, I talk to a couple high yield debt lenders, and after evaluating the company's past cash flows, they are willing to lend another $10M at a higher

---

[41] Simply put, a "tender offer" is the price at which an investor offers current shareholders to sell their stock. Tender offers usually are offered at a premium to market price.

[42] "Collateral" is an asset that is pledged as security for a loan. If the borrower defaults on the loan (doesn't pay it back or doesn't pay it back to the agreed upon terms) the lender may have a right to some or all of the collateral (e.g. if I don't pay my mortgage, the bank gets to take my house)

interest rate[43] than what I'm getting from the bank. This higher interest rate is designed to account for the additional risk in the loan since there is no collateral.

Now that I have my $100M, I go to the owners, buy the company, and begin to use my financial and operational expertise to increase the company's revenue and profitability, so that I can service the debt that was used to finance the acquisition.

In this example, here is the breakdown of the acquisition:

Type of Financing	Value	% of Total
Senior Debt	$80M	80
High Yield Debt	$10M	10
Equity (my money)	$10M	10

Figure Ten: Debt vs. Equity

---

[43] This kind of loan is commonly referred to as a "junk bond."

There are several different strategies for increasing profitability within the acquired business, but for the sake of simplicity, watch what happens if a couple years go by, and the acquired business has successfully paid off the senior debt without much change in the overall value of the company (the company is still worth $100M, but now there's no bank debt).

Type of Financing	Value	% of Total
Senior Debt 2.0	$0M	0
High Yield Debt	$10M	10
Equity (my money) 2.0	$90M	90

Figure Eleven: Debt vs. Equity 2.0

Just like that, I've made $80M on paper! Now, since this is a private investment, I won't actually realize a return on the investment (ROI) until a liquidity event occurs, usually through selling the company.

Strategies:

In the above example, I mentioned that there are a couple different strategies private equity investors use to increase profitability. Although this is not an exhaustive list, here are the most common strategies used by private equity investors[44] to increase the profitability of an acquired business.

---

[44] Please note that usually, a private equity investor simultaneously engages in multiple strategies with the acquired business. For example, a private equity investor may do a breakup for certain

- Breakup
    - A breakup occurs when a private equity investor purchases a large company and sells its various assets / divisions for a total that was greater than the original purchase price.
    - This means that it is possible that the parts be worth a greater amount than the sum, and this can be true. The reason this can be true is that some assets can be sold to strategic buyers for more than the present market value, since the strategic buyers will recognize synergies that are not calculated into the present market value.

- Turnaround
    - "A turnaround is the financial recovery of a company that has been performing poorly for an extended time"[45]
    - Usually, a turnaround is performed by changing the management of the company. A turnaround can also occur by changing the overall company strategy (e.g. stop entering new markets, but instead, focus on improving current product lines).

- Roll-Up Mergers (aka Add-On Mergers)
    - A roll-up occurs when the PE firm seeks several businesses within the same industry, purchases the businesses individually, and then merges the companies together.
    - By merging several small businesses, the PE firm is able to then sell the new, merged company to a larger, strategic buyer.

---

portions of the business, perform a turnaround for the core components of the business, and then exit by performing a reverse LBO.

[45] Definition comes from the following website: http://www.investopedia.com/terms/t/turnaround.asp

- This makes the acquisition sizeable enough to be completed by a larger company, whereas before the PE Investor was involved, the larger company would not have been able to recognize the opportunity (or the larger company would have decided to wait for a PE Investor to get involved, since the larger company is focused on things other than going on an M&A spree).
- Roll-Ups are typically a popular method of consolidating highly fragmented industries.

- Reverse Leveraged Buyout (RLBO)
  - A RLBO is when a PE Investor buys a public company using leverage, holds it as a private entity for a period of time, makes changes to the company while its being held as a private entity, and then sells the equity through an IPO on a stock exchange.
- Secondary Sale
  - A secondary sale is when a Private Equity Investor purchases a company and then sells it to another Private Equity Investor.

Concluding Remarks

Private equity is a field that is oftentimes associated with investment banking, and this is because a significant portion of private equity investors had previously worked in banking. Why banking? One primary reason is that investment banking teaches the financial modeling skills that are necessary to perform leveraged buyout analysis.

What's the difference between venture capital and private equity? Venture capital is characterized by investments in startups, whereas private equity is characterized by acquisitions of mature companies. Venture capital investors take much more risk in their investments and can sometimes be compensated with astronomical returns, whereas private equity investors typically do not take a significant amount of risk in their investments and are usually compensated with moderate / large returns[46].

---

[46] Please note that although I have referred to the returns by PE investors as moderate / large returns when compared to the returns of some venture capital investors, these returns are usually huge when compared to the ROI generated through public investment opportunities, such as the stock market.

Part Four: The "Path"

Figure Twelve: The Path to Your Gated Villa

Every career is unique: not every financier goes down the exact same path.
However, there are a couple of common themes seen within the industry, and by

identifying these common themes, we are able to explain the overarching paths that most people travel along.

Now, on entry-level careers in the financial services industry, there is a route which is very common amongst *some* of the best and brightest graduates of Harvard College and other Ivy League schools.

On the investment banking route, the common themes are as follows:

- The vast majority of graduates moving into investment banking at a bulge bracket bank[47] had previously worked as an intern, at that same investment bank, the summer after their junior year of college.
- The majority of those working at an investment bank are not working for the firm five years later. This happens for a number of reasons, but primarily, it seems that most bankers offer a two-year contract for their analyst program. After two years, the contract is up. Some people will be promoted to the associate program, other people leave to work on the buy-side, and other people go to business school.

Most people who achieve an entry-level position in the financial services industry do NOT stay with their first firm for the long-haul. Now then, why is it that most people do not seem to start a career with their entry-level firm? Let's first examine this question from the firm's point of view, and then let's look at why, even with having this knowledge, many people still choose to accept these careers.

---

[47] Think Big Bank. E.g. Goldman Sachs, JP Morgan, etc.

From the Firm's Point of View:

Bulge Bracket Banks are extremely large organizations. For example, Goldman Sachs employs approximately 34,400 people[48]. These firms, like any for-profit organization in a capitalist society, want to make as much money as possible. The best way to make money is to have ongoing and continuous business, so that more sales can be generated. Since these firms primarily sell services[49], a large number of man-power is needed to generate the services sold.

Let's take a look at an investment bank. An investment bank makes money on advising corporations on strategic M&A deals (Mergers and Acquisitions). The bank usually takes a percentage of the total transaction: the bank makes money when one company acquires another company. A bank can advise a corporate client on an acquisition. To do so, the investment bank must show, usually in the form of a PowerPoint presentation, how the acquisition is beneficial to the client. Preparing the PowerPoint with images, text, and most importantly, a wide arrange of financial models, takes hours of time. To lower the total amount of time, a number of people can work on specific parts of the presentation together. If total time is lowered, more presentations are given, which naturally leads to more sales.

So, why do these firms continuously hire freshly minted college graduates? In short, the firms need to create a ton of PowerPoint Presentations. The jobs are more complex than a simple PowerPoint, and usually include very intense

---

[48] http://www.goldmansachs.com/media-relations/press-releases/current/pdfs/2016-q4-results.pdf
[49] Some firms, and especially banks, like to call a number of their services "products". For the purpose of simplicity, I will refer to these firms as businesses in the service industry, since their "products" are unique and greatly dependent on the specific needs of their clients.

financial modeling, but the gist of it is, a lot of PowerPoints need to be made. So then, why recent college graduates?

1) Recent college graduates are relatively cheap. It's much more affordable to pay a "low" salary to somebody young who likely has no dependents. As somebody becomes more senior, their salary is expected to increase. Instead of paying the increases in salary, it makes more sense to have short-term (2–3 year) programs and get fresh blood into the organization as opposed to support more senior workers.

2) The actual work isn't that difficult. These firms have training programs in which they teach the basic skills, but the majority of college graduates are likely qualified for these jobs.

3) Recent college graduates are flexible. Many banks require long hours that can frequently go past midnight. Since there is no family waiting at home, sacrificing nights is not a problem.

At this point, you may be asking yourself "Okay, so if all I'm doing is making PowerPoint Presentations, why would I want to work an entry-level career in the financial services industry?" To answer this, let's take a look into the student's point of view.

From the Student's Point of View:

The reasons for interviewing for and eventually accepting an entry-level career in the financial services industry go beyond compensation, although compensation is typically high. Bulge bracket banks will pay a $85K+ salary with bonuses that will bring total compensation above $100K for the first year. Beyond compensation, here are some reasons to pursue an entry-level position in the financial services industry:

1) Being one of the few who make the promotions and climb the corporate ladder. This is also highly dependent on luck, since most individual success is directly related to the Managing Director or Partner who is the supervisor for the individual. A rock star MD or Partner that is selling services above the firm average is sure to be doing something right, and getting lucky to work with one of these individuals could be a game-changer for the knowledge and skills learned while on the job.

2) Getting to the buy-side. Most college graduates do not have the skills necessary to work on the buy side immediately after school, and this is due to buy side firms typically being smaller shops that do not offer formal training programs. Instead, buy side firms like to recruit people with previous experience in financial modeling, primarily from investment banks.

3) Going to graduate school but believe it's best to take time-off. Almost all business schools require work experience, and many law schools are starting to take a similar stance on the issue of working before graduate school. This is also an opportunity for students to repay student debt incurred in undergraduate study before potentially racking up more debt by pursuing an advanced degree.

4) Master financial modeling and have deal exposure. If you plan on having a lengthy career in business, getting your start at a bank is not a bad idea.

You'll be exposed to a number of deals and have the opportunity to work with Fortune 500 CEOs.

5) Brand Name Effect. Working for a large firm sticks a gold star on a resume. Working at Goldman Sachs shows that you were qualified to work a top job.

6) Job Security. Most Bulge Bracket banks will hire somebody in the fall of their junior year, the intern will then work for the bank and 90% of the time, the intern receives a return-offer to come back. It's much easier to start senior year with a job in hand rather than frantically searching the market.

7) Learning how to work efficiently. I once had a boss, named Brice, that used to say "every single American College Graduate working in business should be required to do a year at an investment bank." Brice believes that banks teach people a kind of discipline and work ethic that cannot be learned at other places– no other kind of firm will typically require 100+ hour weeks under tremendous pressure. Banks are infamous for being extremely strict on both quantity and quality of work: every number in the model, every word in the text, and every picture's position on a particular slide must be correct.

The Outcome

"The path" followed to a T involves the following steps and begins very early in life. Our experience has shown that steps can be missed along the way, but this may make some opportunities more difficult to be achieved.

1) Graduating in the top decile of your private high school or valedictorian or salutatorian from your public high school.

2) Attending an Ivy League school, Stanford, MIT, CalTech, Boston College, Georgetown, University of Chicago or a handful of other top tier American universities and majoring in a respected discipline (think economics, engineering, applied math, finance, accounting, or history).

3) Interning at a bulge bracket bank in the investment banking division the summer before your junior year.

4) Receiving a full-time offer, graduating from college, and then securing your private equity offer within the first six months of your job at the investment bank.

5) Finishing off the two years of the analyst program, quitting the investment bank, and beginning two years of work at a PE firm.

6) Gaining admission to and attending Harvard Business School, Stanford Graduate School of Business, Wharton, Stern, Yale, Kellogg, Booth, Sloan, Columbia or Ross School of Business.

7) Going right back to private equity at another firm, working your way up the ladder, and retiring on a beach in Tahiti with four Maseratis, a French Chateau, and a platinum jet ski. Yes, you got an A+ in life. Bravo[50].

---

[50] As someone who has personally strayed from the path during step four, I realize that there are many other options than the cookie-cutter version above (and to be fair, I can only personally speak tongue-in-cheek about the path now). An analyst experience at an investment bank or a highly regarded MBA can be used for so much more than just a platform for a PE job. On a

serious note, my life advice to you is never to feel that you should continue down the above path if it is not for you. I personally chose to pursue a more entrepreneurial and academic route than that above; that said, I believe my time as a summer and full-time analyst enabled me to realize what I did and did not want to do with my life. Had I not worked hard at the beginning of this path, other opportunities that have opened up further along it would have never been available to me, even if they did end up taking me far from the well-trod road to success to a more uncertain, but far more exciting highway.

Figure Thirteen: Interviewing

Part Five: Job Information

Overview: Junior-Senior Summer Internship Recruiting

The primary goal of every aspiring investment banker should be to secure an internship at his or her target bank for the summer between junior and senior year. Generally speaking, 50-90% of summer analysts in IBD will be offered full-time positions. Of these, a large majority will either accept their initial offers, or use these offers as leverage to secure a spot at another, perhaps better bank. For those students who intern at large hedge funds or large private equity firms the summer before their senior years, if they receive offers back, it is much easier to use these as leverage for other PE firms or HFs with similar strategies than it is for students in banking to leverage theirs for jobs at other IBs. The reason for this is that PE firms and HFs hire talent, whereas IBs hire workhorses. The ability to work long hours doing (relatively) unskilled work is far more commoditized than actual skill (which is what PE firms and HFs try to recruit)[51]. At any rate, the hardworking summer analyst will have a job offer in hand by mid-August and will be able to spend his or her senior year either 1) leveraging an offer to secure a better job 2) taking meaningful classes without really worrying about GPA 3) applying themselves wholeheartedly to a thesis project or 4) kicking back and enjoying life before having to enter the real world.

---

[51] The caveat to this is that if a student interns at a very specific HF or PE firm (for example, a quantitative hedge fund), it is very unlikely that the student will be able to leverage that offer as well at a fund with a different strategy. Alternatively, I personally have seen students who had previously little financial experience but superior academic abilities use their offers from bulge brackets as leverage to obtain offers from buy-side firms after junior-senior summer.

From the time a rising junior has her first investment banking internship interview with the firm that eventually hires her to the time she first steps foot into the office as a full-time analyst, two years elapse. Yes, you read that correctly: to secure an investment banking job at a bulge bracket bank, you have to be prepared two years in advance of when you start the full-time job. The job recruiting process (especially for investment banks) is a far cry from the days when students dialed up companies in the phone book a day after graduating and asked if there were openings. Furthermore, the application, interview, and offer process have become far more streamlined in the past two to three years than they had been previously. In the next chapter, I will demonstrate how and why the banking recruiting process has become accelerated. In Chapter 11, I will highlight the steps necessary to secure an internship for junior-senior summer. In Chapter 12, I have included a resume and email template that many successful applicants have used.

Chapter 10: The Recruiting Timeline (the Brief History of a Brief Acceleration)

I once worked for a professor of finance who told me that the day after she graduated college, she and the rest of her classmates went through the phone book and called up every company they thought might hire them. That was over 20 years ago when there were fewer opportunities for students to intern anywhere, let alone at investment banks. Five years ago, it was very rare for there to be any final round (or super-day) interviews in the fall. Generally, banks came on-campus[52] for networking events in mid-to-late fall. Students would speak with representatives, receive business cards, and follow up with those professionals to whom they had spoken, in the hopes of their resumes being lifted from the stack of literally thousands that were submitted before the early January deadlines. When students came back to campus a week before second semester began, they would have a week of first-round interviews where they would be evaluated against their peers from the same university. After first-round interviews[53], an email notification would inform the applicant whether she had made it to the second-round, which was generally the final round. If the student had successfully made it to the next-round, the bank would usually assign someone from that university's recruiting team (an alumnus or alumna of the college) to call the student and make sure they were at least minimally prepared for the final-round or superday. Having read up and prepared extensively for the final round, the student would then be flown in and put up in a hotel the night before the superday. The following morning, the banker hopeful would arrive at the New York office in a tie and pinned-on smile to hide the nerves she undoubtedly felt. Generally, the interviewee would meet

---

[52] Here I am describing the on-campus recruiting processes for target colleges.
[53] Which are generally conducted by alumni who now work at the firm.

with the campus recruiting team who had given her the go-ahead to get to the final round. After having lunch with the team, the interviewee would be interviewed in three 30-minute interviews structured in either one-one-one or two-on-one formats. After the interviews, the student, feeling exhausted, dazed, but hopefully not confused, would board a plane home. In about a week, she would find out by phone call whether or not she got the job.

Fast forward five years. First round interviews are now conducted in August, with the opportunity for diversity program applicants to interview before those who go through the normal application process. Offers can be handed out as soon as September. Before the first of the fall networking events, many students already have offers. Why have things been sped up this much? Banks compete for the best candidates. If Goldman Sachs hands out offers in October, the student who receives one is more likely to take it than risk allowing it to expire[54] while waiting on a final interview status from another firm. As one bank moves up, they all move up. Additionally, if a bank has an earlier recruiting program, they allow themselves to scoop up the best and most prepared students. Some argue that by moving the process earlier, banks risk losing out on talented students who are perhaps unsure of whether or not they want to enter the field and have not committed time to preparing for the interview. From the perspective of those in charge of campus recruiting, this is not a valid argument—banks only want to recruit people who are capable of hitting deadlines on time and are truly committed to the job. In their eyes, students who wait are marginal applicants who would probably quit after two years in the analyst program anyway. Additionally,

---

[54] Oftentimes banks give "exploding offers" with a set expiration date so that students act quickly, and so banks can fill their analyst classes sooner rather than later.

it is much easier for HR if they can staff an intern class sooner rather than later—the quicker they get their job done, the earlier they can go on vacation.

Chapter 11: The Recruiting Timeline

Late Summer / Early Fall Recruiting

Ideally, by the final days of your sophomore year, you have decided definitively whether or not you want to intern for an investment bank next summer. Even if you are not sure of whether or not you want to devote your life, or even your early 20s to finance, you still need to figure out your plans for what you will be doing 365 days from now. If you decide a year from now you want to work for an IB after graduation, but your junior-senior summer you decided to work at a startup isolating grasshopper protein for bodybuilder shakes, you are probably out of luck unless your dad is drinking buddies with Mr. Blankfein[55]. In the case that you do in fact want to work for an investment bank next summer, you need to get your stuff together, and by stuff, I mean your 1) list of contacts 2) calendar of any and all application deadlines and networking events 3) finance-oriented resume 4) elevator pitch and 5) interview question answers.

If you are an athlete on a varsity sports team, hit up former teammates working at firms to which you are applying. Ask them to put you in contact with HR. If you do this early enough in the summer, HR will sometimes invite you to summer summits at the bank which are in reality an opportunity for the firm to have early access to top talent and a chance to screen potential applicants. Make a list of friends who have gone on to work for reputable companies and make sure you let them know that you want to work there as well. As you attend networking

---

[55] We are partly kidding with this; most analyst spots for bulge bracket banks are already filled by this point, but opportunities still exist at boutiques.

events in autumn, expand this contact list to include professionals you meet at these events.

Networking Events:

The logistics regarding these events are generally found on the college's career services page. For many reasons, the events listed here might be partially incorrect, so always contact campus recruiting at the target investment bank to ensure that you attend the proper event and understand which divisions will be represented. Oftentimes, there are events not listed on the career's site, but if you inquire with an actual human at the bank, they will be willing to share the information with you. Personally, when I was applying to sales and trading jobs, I particularly wanted to work for Goldman Sachs. On Harvard's career services page, I spotted a networking event for GS's markets division on campus. Because the event occurred at an odd time of the day, very few students showed up to the event, and the few that did had very little idea about what this division did, and much less about how to dress for a financial networking session[56]. The trader at the event and I hit it off, particularly because 1) I had dressed appropriately 2) had asked **relevant questions**[57] about his job and 3) came off as likeable and easy to talk to. I stayed to speak with him after the event had officially ended, and he let

---

[56] For young men, the proper attire is a dark suit, ironed shirt, dark leather shoes, and a tie (optional). For young women, I found the most successful wearing suit jackets and knee-length skirts.

[57] Relevant networking questions should 1) demonstrate a high-level knowledge of the business 2) a prior interest in what the professional does and 3) ask for information unavailable online. Asking the representative "do you like your job" is a poor question. Asking a derivatives salesperson "how much time do you spend with clients per week" is a decent question. Asking a banker "is there a particular reason you selected to cover TMT/Industrials/Real Estate" is a very good question.

me know there was an exclusive networking session being held off campus at a bar in a week's time. I proceeded to attend two more networking sessions with the folks at GS which enabled me to skip the first round of interviews and head straight to superday. Throughout the entire networking process, I stuck to a fluid version of my **elevator pitch**. An elevator pitch is a 30-60 second summary of who you are, where you come from, and how you fit in at the firm / what value you might add. An elevator pitch is like a verbal business card that the people with whom you speak will pack away mentally in the compartment that also stores your name and face. An example elevator pitch is demonstrated below.

Elevator Pitch:

I'm a junior at Brown. I'm originally from Hanover, New Hampshire and I'm the goalie on the varsity soccer team. I study economics and math, and I'm a teaching assistant for two of the lower level calculus courses. Last summer I interned for a small hedge fund that traded volatility. The traders there taught me all about the Greeks[58] and I helped them out by creating a program in Python that priced simple exotics like barrier options and digitals. I really liked what I did there, but I realized I wanted to work for a bigger company with a potential to do more than just option pricing. I also realized that although I liked the trading floor at the hedge fund, I also wanted to work with clients, which you tend to do more of on the sell side.

---

[58] The main Greeks are Delta, Vega, Theta, and Rho. These respectively measure the sensitivity of an option's price with respect to change in price of the underlying security, change in volatility, change in time to expiry, and change in interest rates. This information is just included for your edification; you don't need to know it if you're interested in traditional investment banking. That said, using these terms correctly exemplifies insider knowledge.

Fall or early Winter Interviews

After networking like a boss, you should be able to ensure that you pass the first resume screen to secure a first-round interview. Generally, these first-round interviews are either conducted 1) via phone by a junior professional at the firm or 2) in-person at a branch office close to campus. These interviews are generally less about fit and more about screening out people who are obviously incapable or unsuitable for the job. In these interviews, you are expected to ace every technical question[59] (which demonstrates you actually care about getting the job and have a baseline of competence to perform) and that you would not be a weird personality type at the firm[60]. No matter what the firm, interviews will include at least one of the questions: 1) walk me through your resume 2) tell me about yourself 3) why should we hire you? All of these questions either explicitly or implicitly require you to refer to your resume for demonstrable examples of your viability as a job candidate. We have included a resume template in the next chapter, but the primary rule of resumes is as follows: ***DON'T LIE!*** Resume padding is very common, and in a world in which only the shiniest resumes get past initial screenings, it definitely behooves aspiring bankers to put their best feet forward, but it is essential that students do not list 1) positions they do not hold 2) inflated job titles or 3) skills they cannot replicate in an interview. HR often calls former employers or college clubs and inquires whether or not an applicant holds the title affixed to the organization in a resume. This can be problematic if two people submit resumes to the same firm and both claim to hold the same position in the

---

[59] Technical questions are questions that exemplify a more than superficial understanding of the specific work investment bankers perform.

[60] By weird, I mean here one of 1) an obvious finance douche (no one likes a douchebag) 2) extremely shy or flighty or 3) someone who shows anxiety under pressure.

club—the contender will get passed through the screening, and the pretender will get tossed out. If an interviewee claims to have intimate and deep knowledge of a skill they only understand superficially, he or she runs the risk of being asked to replicate the skill in the interview[61]. This can lead to the interviewee appearing like a fish out of water, or a dog with its head stuck in a hole (see the infographic on the next page).

Granted you do not make yourself look like a turkey[62] (gobble, gobble![63]) in the first-round, you should receive a call from your first-round interviewers congratulating you on moving to the next round. The next round is generally the final round or superday. As I described in the overview, these interviews consist of three 30-minute sessions and will leave even the most prepared interviewee at least a bit tired by the end. Generally, these interviews are a mix of fit and technical questions. Even though you have already demonstrated your technical ability at the first-round, senior bankers who have not already seen you will still try to vet out those interviewees whose backgrounds seem 1) overly inflated or 2) technically soft. A word of caution regarding those of you who come from elite universities—if you come from a top-top-tier college, you may have a metaphorical target on your head in an interview if the interviewer had to claw his or her way to the top from a second-tier school. In this situation, the interviewer is primed to see you as a cocky, over-privileged rich kid, even if your background is growing up on the dirt floor of a cow farm. The interviewer might envy your position, and if you occasion them an opportunity to strike you down with an

---

[61] This is especially true for someone who claims to be professionally proficient in a foreign language.

[62] A "turkey" is New England slang for an idiot.

[63] I acknowledge that this is the least interesting part of the book to read (and also to write), but please push through because there is very important logistical information lodged in these next few pages.

impossible technical question, he or she will surely pounce like a self-made and frustrated viper. To avoid this outcome, make sure to word answers such that they cannot be construed as high-flown or snobbish. Additionally, do not make reference to ideas or concepts you do not know perfectly. For example, if you talk about wanting to work for a bank's leveraged finance group (known as "Lev Fin" to those in the know), but you do not know the least bit about how a leveraged buyout model (LBO) works, you are probably going to disqualify yourself from the job if the interviewer asks you to explain how the model works. A full list of potential interview questions for each role in finance is beyond the scope of this book[64].

---

[64] At the time of this edition's publication, Morgan Eldon is considering offering consulting services which would include, among other things, an exhaustive list of interview questions and answers.

Figure Fourteen: Rare Photo of Banking Interviewee Caught Lying in Interview

Accepting the Offer

After those three 30-minute sessions, you will quickly email your interviewers with thank you emails (that are personalized, and never cookie-cutter). They will take a general form of something like the following, but should include specifics discussed in the interview.

Follow-up Thank You Email:

Hello Jane,

It was great meeting and interviewing with you today. I'm very excited about the possibility of working at Global Investment Bank and I think I would be a very good fit for the firm. You and everyone else I met today have reinforced the impression that not only will I be able to grow a successful career at Global Investment Bank, but that I will be able to do it in a culture[65] that I would enjoy being a part of.

Thanks so much,
Morgan

If you are successful at superday, one of the interviewers will call you in the next few to several days to let you know you have the internship. Oftentimes, the person calling will ask you if you would take the job immediately (i.e. confirm

---

[65] Jane mentioned culture in the interview, so a specific mention of the topic discussed helps you avoid sounding like you are using a cookie-cutter email.

officially on the phone) if it were offered you. What you do not want to do in this situation is panic. By the time offers come out, you should know where firms rank in terms of your preferences. If the firm calling you is your first choice, by all means, accept on the phone. It is generally impossible to negotiate terms of an internship, so do not think that being coy will help you. If the firm calling is not your top choice, and you are still waiting on the result of another firm, it is perfectly ok to tell the caller that you are excited about the opportunity, but want to talk to your career advisor or college advisor about it before making a decision. You do not need to mention the specifics of other companies at which you interviewed. The worst thing to do is renege an offer, or accept and then withdraw. This reduces your credibility and comes off as lying—do not do this if avoidable. Make sure you sign on the dotted line and secure a contract before withdrawing other applications.

Chapter 12: Resume Template

BANKY B. BANKSTER

bankybankster@college.dartvard.edu ▪ 555-123-4567

101 Partridge Mail Center, Cambridge   11 Bank Street, Michelin
New Hampshire 02888   Massachusetts 02222

EDUCATION

DARTVARD COLLEGE   **CAMBRIDGE, NEW HAMPSHIRE**
A.B. Candidate in Applied Mathematics   *AUGUST, 2015—PRESENT*
- GPA: 3.5/4.0
- Relevant Coursework: Economics 1111 (Corporate Finance), Math 66 (Quantitative Finance and Modeling), Accounting 243 (Graduate Level Financial Accounting)

SALMON SHORTS ACADEMY   **GREENWICH, CONNECTICUT**
Salutatorian of the Class of 2015   *AUGUST, 2011—MAY, 2015*
- GPA: 4.0/4.0; SAT: 2320/2400
- Honors: 2015 Super Salmon of the Year, National French Exam Level VI-Connecticut First Place, Varsity Rowing Captain, Mathlete of the Year 2014

PROFESSIONAL EXPERIENCE

HONEY BADGER CAPITAL   **BOSTON, MASSACHUSETTS**
QUANTITATIVE TRADING SUMMER ANALYST   *MAY, 2017—AUGUST, 2017*
Small investment management company punching above its weight in options trading.
- Conducted backtesting on convertible arbitrage strategies.
- Utilized object-oriented programming languages to develop an exotic options pricer.

THE MATH ACADEMY   **GREENWICH, CONNECTICUT**
MATH INSTRUCTOR AND MENTOR   *JUNE, 2014—MAY, 2017*
- Tutored Calculus I to rising high school seniors and developed a curriculum to prepare students to skip Pre-Calculus.
- Led SAT II preparation class to increase students' scores on the Math I and Math II SAT subject tests; students achieved a mean score increase of 150 points.
- Trained new hires on curriculum building to increase their progression from junior tutor to full tutor; all new hires advanced three months ahead of schedule.

LEADERSHIP & ACTIVITIES

DARTVARD INVESTMENT SOCIETY   **CAMBRIDGE, NEW HAMPSHIRE**
TREASURER   *SEPTEMBER, 2016—PRESENT*
Dartvard's foremost undergraduate financial club. Provides instruction in the basics of finance and manages a fund with $180k AUM.
- Manage the club's operating expenses, assist in teaching the investment class, and apply for grants.
- Led a group of first-year club members in pitching Chipotle for final project stock pitch; all group members passed and were admitted to the club.

DARTVARD VARSITY ROWING   **CAMBRIDGE, NEW HAMPSHIRE**
ATHLETE   *AUGUST, 2015—PRESENT*
- Commit 25-30 hours a week to practice in pursuit of a league title.

ADDITIONAL INFORMATION

Technical Training: Python, Java, Stata, Microsoft Office
Languages: English (native fluency) • French (professional fluency)
Interests: Rowing, Fishing, Music, Travel

114

Closing Remarks

Having read everything above, you should now at least know if this path is definitely not for you. If you have decided that investment banking is for the birds, good—you can forget about applying to these jobs and move on with your colorful, non-Excel based life. For those of you who remain intrigued, we strongly urge you to learn more before applying. Once you have made your decision (and we urge you not to take this decision lightly) of what you want to do with your early 20s, use our experiences to your benefit. Good luck!

Appendix I: Real-World Example of an IPO

Snap Inc. is a camera company that owns the mobile application Snapchat. To help finance business operations, Snap raised $3.4 Billion through an Initial Public Offering (IPO) of its stock on March 2, 2017. In this example, Snap is a *user of capital*.

How did Snap raise $3.4 Billion exactly? A number of investment banks including Morgan Stanley and Goldman Sachs underwrote the IPO, which means they helped Snap sell shares on a public stock exchange, in this case specifically, the New York Stock Exchange.

How it Works: after a number of investor presentations occur, known as roadshows, the investment banks determine a price for which they are willing to purchase stock directly from the company. The company sells the stock to the bank, and then the bank sells the stock to other investors. Since the bank's primary task is unloading the assets, i.e. selling the stock to investors on a public exchange, the bank is called a sell-side firm. The investors who purchase Snap stock from the bank, which are usually mutual funds, are buy-side firms.

Additional Info: The company wants to work with investment banks for two primary reasons: 1) working with an investment bank can guarantee the company is able to raise money, since the bank may be purchasing the shares directly and 2) the investment bank has expert knowledge on how to sell shares in accordance with SEC Regulations. Once the investment bank feels that the market is ready, the bank buys the shares from the company and then immediately sells them to a variety of investors. In this example, the bank purchases the shares since it has made a firm commitment.

Notes

www.ingramcontent.com/pod-product-compliance
Lightning Source LLC
Chambersburg PA
CBHW081731220526
45468CB00008B/2058